Foreword

The recent emphasis on the high cost of health care has led many commentators to identify expenditure restraint as the main objective of OECD governments seeking to reform their health systems. To the contrary, cost-effectiveness (the delivery of appropriate, quality health services at the lowest possible cost) is the main focus of recent health reforms within OECD countries.

After two decades of priority given to extending access to medical services, OECD countries started, in the early 1980s, to focus on making their health systems more efficient. To that effect, most countries initially emphasised the aggregate control of the use of resources. However, they found that achieving this goal of macroeconomic efficiency may conflict with microeconomic objectives. As a result, in the late 1980s and early 1990s there has been a blossoming of innovative reforms in an attempt to achieve microeconomic efficiency too. In many countries, governments have concluded that an extensive bureaucratisation of the health delivery and financing institutions (developed in the pursuit of extended access and global budget control) was counterproductive. The introduction of incentive mechanisms which have worked well in the business sector has been the central characteristic common to these recent health system innovations. At the same time, mainly for reasons of equity, health systems have remained predominantly publicly funded.

Previous publications in this series produced evidence to support the proposition that it is inappropriate, low-quality health services, rather than the pursuit of appropriate services of good quality, that are expensive. This volume adds to that evidence. It consists of chapters from three recent economic surveys which were prepared by the OECD's Economics Department for the Economic and Development Review Committee: the United Kingdom (July 1994), Canada (November 1993) and Iceland (May 1993). There is a common message in these country experiences: investment in the delivery of health services needs to be balanced against the expected benefits of that investment. Evidence suggests that progress in advancing medical technology has been faster than the development of techniques to measure the effectiveness of these new procedures. This has made it more difficult to steer resources towards productive uses and away from inefficiency and waste. At the same time, the available evidence for these three countries also highlights some fast successes of the reforms. The evidence to date suggests that gains in effectiveness have been considerable in some areas of health reform.

These three national case studies, which were initially part of the regular economic surveys of these countries, demonstrate a convergence of the objectives of macroeconomic management and of health policy formulation which is occurring across countries. This report is published on the responsibility of the Secretary-General of the OECD.

T.J. Alexander
Director for Education, Employment,
Labour and Social Affairs

3

ALSO AVAILABLE

Series OECD Social Policy Studies:

Health Care Systems in Transition: The Search for Efficiency, No. 7 (1990)
(81 89 05 1) ISBN 92-64-13310-0
France: FF140   Other countries: FF180 US$30.00 DM55

New Orientations for Social Policy, No. 12 (1994)
(81 94 02 1) ISBN 92-64-14056-5
France: FF120   Other countries: FF155 US$26.00 DM46

Series OECD Health Policy Studies:

US Health Care at the Cross-Roads, No. 1 (1992)
(11 92 03 1) ISBN 92-64-13780-7
France: FF60   Other countries: FF80 US$9.00 DM25

The Reform of Health Care: A Comparative Analysis of Seven OECD Countries, No. 2 (1992)
(81 92 02 1) ISBN 92-64-13791-2
France: FF180   Other countries: FF230 US$46.00 DM74

OECD Heath Systems: Facts and Trends 1960-1991, No. 3, 2 volumes (1993)
(81 93 05 1) ISBN 92-64-13800-5
France: FF380   Other countries: FF475 US$89.00 DM150

Health: Quality and Choice, No. 4 (1994)
(81 94 01 1) ISBN 92-64-14213-4
France: FF120   Other countries: FF155 US$28 DM47

The Reform of Health Care Systems: A Review of Seventeen OECD Countries, No. 5 (1994)
(81 94 10 1) ISBN 92-64-14250-9
France: FF375   Other countries: FF470 US$86 DM142

Prices charged at the OECD Bookshop.
THE OECD CATALOGUE OF PUBLICATIONS and supplements will be sent free of charge
on request addressed either to OECD Publications Service,
or to the OECD Distributor in your country.

Table of contents

Chapter 1

UNITED KINGDOM

Chapter 2

CANADA

Chapter 3

ICELAND

List of Tables

List of Diagrams

Chapter 1

UNITED KINGDOM

Introduction

Roughly three years have passed since a number of important reform measures were introduced to the UK national health service (NHS). These reforms sought to increase the flexibility and efficiency of the system and to enhance the quality of health care. They attempt to accomplish this by creating market-like competition for purchasing and providing certain types of hospital and community health services.[1] This chapter first puts UK health spending in an international perspective and describes the characteristics of the UK health care system. The key elements of the reform are then presented and the main changes in the system since the reform discussed. Finally, the chapter evaluates what remains to be done in light of how the system has evolved to date in response to the reforms.

UK health care spending: international comparisons

In 1992, the United Kingdom spent £42 billion on health care, representing 6.7 per cent of trend GDP (Table 1.1). This compares with an average share of health spending in GDP of 8.2 per cent in the OECD as a whole in 1992, and 7.5 per cent in the European Community. As in many other OECD countries, particularly outside North America, the UK ratio of health spending to GDP generally stabilised in the first half of the 1980s following significant growth in the 1970s. Since 1985, this ratio

Table 1.1. **Total health expenditure as percentage of trend GDP**

	1970	1975	1980	1985	1990	1992
United States	7.2	8.1	9.3	10.5	12.3	13.5
Japan	4.6	5.5	6.7	6.5	6.9	7.1
Germany	6.0	7.9	8.7	8.5	8.6	9.1
France	5.9	6.8	7.7	8.2	8.9	9.2
Italy	5.3	5.9	7.1	6.9	8.2	8.4
United Kingdom	4.4	5.4	5.9	5.8	6.3	6.7
Canada	6.9	7.1	7.4	8.4	9.3	9.9
Average of above countries	5.8	6.7	7.5	7.8	8.7	9.1
Australia	6.1	8.1	7.8	8.3	8.2	8.4
Austria	5.4	7.2	8.2	8.0	8.6	8.9
Belgium	4.0	5.7	6.7	7.1	7.7	7.9
Denmark	6.1	6.3	6.8	6.4	6.2	6.4
Finland	5.9	6.4	6.7	7.4	8.4	8.5
Greece	4.1	4.0	4.4	4.9	5.3	5.5
Ireland	5.6	8.0	9.3	7.9	7.0	7.1
Netherlands	6.1	7.3	8.1	7.7	8.3	8.7
Norway	5.0	7.2	6.6	6.6	7.3	7.9
Portugal	3.1	6.1	6.2	6.6	6.6	6.5
Spain	3.7	4.8	5.8	5.5	6.9	7.1
Sweden	7.3	8.0	9.6	9.1	9.1	8.6
European Community	4.9	6.2	7.0	6.9	7.3	7.5
OECD total	5.4	6.6	7.3	7.4	7.9	8.2

Source: OECD.

has increased by nearly 1 percentage point of GDP, with relatively strong growth – above the EC and OECD averages – apparent since 1990.

UK health outcomes appear, for the most part, to be comparable with those achieved in other countries. Data on perinatal and infant mortality, and on potential years of life lost[2] are close to G7 and OECD averages; the same is true of life expectancy at birth and at age 80.[3]

Annual growth rates over the last two decades in per capita health expenditures are shown in Table 1.2. During the 1972-82 period, growth in real health spending (using the GDP deflator) was 3.8 per cent per year, below the EC and OECD averages, but volume growth (column C) moved closer to the OECD average when account is taken of the slightly slower growth in health prices compared with economy-wide prices in the United Kingdom. In 1982-92, real growth in health spending (based on the GDP deflator) was the same as in the preceding decade (but above the EC and OECD averages). However, the rate of increase in "volume" terms was half that of the 1972-82 period, reflecting the fact that "excess" health price inflation grew by 1.7 per cent per year, a relatively strong rate when compared both with the 1970s and with most other countries during the 1980s. Medical health price inflation does not generally take account of productivity gains. As there is some evidence of a recent improvement in productivity in the United Kingdom, at least, the volume deceleration may be exaggerated.[4]

Table 1.2. **Growth rates of per capita health expenditure**

Annual growth rates

	1972-82				1982-92			
	A	B	C	D	A	B	C	D
United States	12.4	4.1	3.3	0.8	8.6	5.1	2.5	2.7
Japan	14.2	6.6	7.4	−0.7	5.5	4.3	3.3	1.0
Germany	9.8	4.8	4.0	0.7	5.4	2.4	2.4	−0.1
France	16.2	4.8	6.5	−1.7	8.0	3.2	4.3	−1.1
Italy	22.5	4.5	4.8	−0.3	12.9	4.4	3.4	1.0
United Kingdom	18.4	3.8	4.0	−0.2	9.5	3.8	2.1	1.7
Canada	13.5	3.7	3.1	0.6	7.7	4.1	2.7	1.4
Average of above countries	15.3	4.6	4.7	−0.1	8.2	3.9	3.0	0.9
Australia	16.0	3.9	2.8	1.1	8.5	2.4	2.6	−0.2
Austria	13.4	6.7	4.3	2.4	6.6	3.1	1.4	1.7
Belgium	15.5	7.8	7.3	0.5	6.7	2.7	1.8	0.9
Denmark	12.5	2.2	2.9	−0.7	5.9	1.6	1.6	0.0
Finland	16.3	3.9	3.9	0.1	9.9	4.3	2.0	2.2
Greece	21.4	3.4	3.2	0.2	21.1	3.3	3.4	−0.1
Iceland	50.5	6.1	5.3	0.8	26.3	1.9	1.9	0.1
Ireland	20.7	5.2	6.6	−1.3	5.9	1.7	−0.7	2.5
Luxembourg	13.6	5.4	7.0	−1.6	7.5	3.7	2.5	1.2
Netherlands	10.8	3.5	1.4	2.1	3.9	2.2	1.7	0.5
Norway	14.9	4.8	4.6	0.1	8.4	4.3	2.4	1.9
Portugal	..	..	..	..	20.8	3.6	5.0	−1.4
Spain	21.3	4.4	4.6	−0.2	13.1	4.5	5.8	−1.3
Sweden	14.5	4.0	3.2	0.9	6.9	0.1	0.5	−0.4
Switzerland	8.3	3.4	1.5	1.9	6.2	2.4	2.2	0.2
New Zealand	16.8	3.3	..	..	9.9	1.7	1.3	0.4
European Community	16.6	4.5	4.8	−0.2	10.1	3.1	2.8	0.3
OECD total	16.2	4.4	4.2	0.2	10.1	3.2	2.5	0.7

A) Nominal growth in per capita health spending.
B) Real (GDP deflator) growth in per capita health spending.
C) Real (medical price deflator) growth in per capita health spending.
D) "Excess" health price inflation: *i.e.* medical price deflator less GDP deflator. It should be noted that medical price inflation is generally measured as the difference between nominal expenditure growth and volume growth. In calculating volume growth of health services, an assumption of zero productivity growth is normally made. There are many indicators (reduction in hospital stays, increases in throughput and the introduction of new technology) which suggest that productivity has improved in many countries. The implication is that the volume of health services has risen faster than suggested in column C and that medical inflation is less than in column D. For evidence on the United Kingdom, see Diagram 1.2.
Source: OECD.

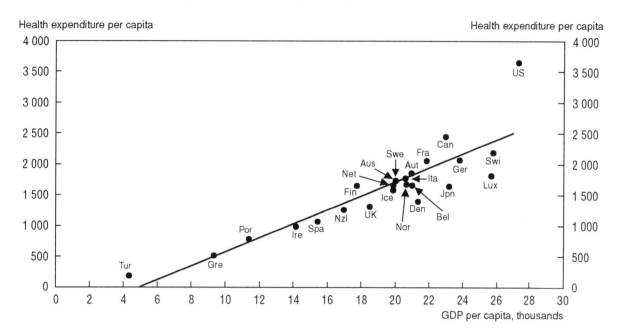

Diagram 1.1. **Health spending versus GDP, 1992**

Note: Data shown are PPPs in US dollars, converted to a price level OECD = 100.
Source: OECD (1992), Purchasing Power Parities and Real Expenditures, and OECD (1993), OECD Health Systems: Facts and Trends, 1960-1991.

International differences in levels of per capita health spending appear to be linked closely to differences in overall income or spending levels.[5] Diagram 1.1 shows per capita health spending related to GDP per capita, where national currency units have been converted to a common currency (US dollar) using GDP purchasing power parities (PPPs). The regression line, which "explains" 78 per cent of the inter-country variation in per capita health spending, suggests that UK health spending per capita is around 14 per cent below its "predicted" level, and substantially below countries such as Australia, Finland, and the Netherlands with similar levels of GDP per capita.

The picture almost certainly changes in the UK's favour when international differences in the prices of medical inputs are taken into account. Tentative estimates of PPPs for health care suggest that the level of UK prices are substantially below the OECD average, while, for example, US prices are significantly above this average. The NHS has several institutional characteristics that have tended to be associated with slower rates of growth in health spending internationally, and which may have helped to produce a lower price structure in the United Kingdom compared with countries with markedly different health systems.[6] It is not clear at this stage whether taking account of relative health prices accounts for some or all of the difference referred to above.

The national health service before reform

The UK national health service emerged in broadly its present form in 1948. Although there have been significant reforms to administrative practices at various times, the essentials of the 1948 scheme remained unchanged for several decades. It was paid for almost exclusively out of general taxation. The Secretary of State was accountable to Parliament for all policy and expenditure. Day-to-day administration was delegated to regional and local bodies, but they were appointed by and accountable to the central government. For hospital and community care services, regional budgets were made on a per capita basis adjusted for demographic and other factors. These regional budgets were passed on to the hospitals and other facilities via district health authorities (DHAs) following similar principles, who then used the money to finance the hospital and community health services they administered. General

11

practitioners were paid under a central contract involving a mixture of capitation, fee for service and other payments, administered by local family health service authorities. A small amount was allocated to GPs from regional budgets to pay towards the cost of practice staff, premises and computers.

Prior to the reforms, the NHS would appear to have been the most highly centralised health care system in the OECD area. Indeed, it remains more centralised and its budget continues to be more closely controlled than under the Spanish and Italian systems, even after reforms in those countries. The UK system also embodied a much cherished principle – free access by all citizens to comprehensive medical care. Over the period since 1948 the principle of free access had been eroded, notably in dental and optical care. By the end of the 1980s such services were charged at near cost, although people over pension age, pregnant women, children, people on low incomes and those with certain medical conditions do not pay. Pharmaceuticals prescribed by family doctors also carried a charge. Yet visits to the doctor and all hospital care and community health services were free of charge.

The UK pattern of health service delivery is broadly similar to those in Canada or the Scandinavian countries, the main difference being that administration and finance in these latter countries were more decentralised. The UK system differs from some continental European systems (such as those of France and Germany) in that it is not based on an insurance scheme that reimburses secondary service providers on a fee-for-service basis. Prior to 1991, hospitals in the United Kingdom (as in most public hospitals elsewhere) received a budget from central government and had to keep within it. If they do not, the responsible managers might be dismissed or otherwise sanctioned, as has sometimes happened. These constraints and sanctions now apply to the district health authorities as purchasers. This capacity to set and to enforce a budget limit distinguishes the UK system from those of other countries where there are many social insurance agencies and many providers and where budgetary or expenditure control is often ineffective.[7] Tight budget control under the national health hervice, however, was obtained through an inflexible system for allocating funds to hospitals and was frequently associated with long queues and with a lack of sensitivity to patients' needs and tastes.

The other important cost saving feature of the UK system is the family doctor or GP. GPs are paid a fixed amount per patient (depending on age) together with certain allowances and fees for services in return for providing (loosely-defined) general medical services for their patients. Patients have a right to choose their GP, but may not have more than one GP at a time. This GP, in addition to providing ambulatory services, acts as a "gate-keeper" for hospital care; that is, he determines whether or not his patients should be admitted to a hospital for non-emergency or "elective" treatment. No hospital will agree to see a patient for elective surgery unless the GP has given the patient a letter of referral.

Nearly the entire British population relies on the NHS for its health care, though private health insurance is also permitted. In the early 1980s the number of privately-insured individuals grew, but later stalled with the recession. In 1988, only about 15 per cent of the population had some form of private health insurance coverage, most of which was for short-term acute hospital care (Propper and Maynard, 1990). On the whole, the NHS system appears to have provided an adequate level of health services for all people who chose to be enrolled in it. Furthermore, the NHS was able to compete effectively with private health services when the prices it charged for its services were set at or near zero. This is admittedly not a very exacting performance standard, but it is not one that all OECD countries' public health services have managed to achieve: in some, the costs of queuing and the uncertainty as to the timing and quality of care have made it hard for the public system to compete, even when the system's explicit charges are far lower than those of private alternatives.[8]

There were good reasons to retain the essential features of the NHS. First, it was, and is, considered by much of the population to be one of the most successful of all British social institutions. Dissatisfaction did increase substantially in the 1980s, as the regular surveys of British Social Attitudes show (Jowell et al., 1991). However, "(...) far from reducing allegiance to the NHS, dissatisfaction appears to fuel demands for extra expenditure and attention" (Taylor-Gooby, 1991, p. 40). Second, the comprehensive access to free medical care provided by the NHS had brought increased equality to the distribution of health care in the decades since the second world war (Propper and O'Donnell, 1991). Third, as the section on international comparisons has shown, the NHS delivered satisfactory health standards for the UK population and was relatively inexpensive (see also Barr et al., 1988). It was, and is, a remarkably cost-effective institution. Fourth, the incentives to supply excessive medical services inherent in many continental European and US systems of health finance were absent. The UK government had powerful and effective means of controlling health costs.

Ironically, it was the major strength of the system – the effectiveness of the budget control process – that played an important role in unleashing the pressure for change. Public spending on

Table 1.3. **Resources and demands of the NHS (Hospital and Community Health Services), 1983-88**

Per cent per annum

	Real purchasing power increase	Increase needed for demographic change	Real net plus/minus
1983/84	0	0.9	−0.9
1984/85	−0.1	0.9	−1.0
1985/86	0.5	1.1	−0.6
1986/87	0.6	0.8	−0.2
1987/88	1.9	1.5	0.4

Source: H.M. Treasury and Department of Health and Social Welfare.

health grew substantially more slowly in the 1980s than in the preceding decade and a half relative to GDP. Under Mrs. Thatcher's administration, the rate of growth for total public spending grew broadly in line with GDP in the first half of the decade and somewhat less for inpatient care. But growth was particularly slow from FY 1983/84 on, as tight cash limits began to bite (Table 1.3). These tight limits coincided with a growth in the very elderly population and a revival in the number of births. This, in turn, was reflected in a real decline in spending per head of the cost-weighted population and a resource crunch ensued. The experience of the 1980s underscored the limits of a policy of reducing health expenditure while leaving the institutions of health care delivery untouched. It therefore shifted the policy focus toward systemic reform.

The command-and-control system of the NHS lacked flexibility, incentives for efficiency, financial information (and hence accountability) and choice of providers of secondary care. A prominent American health economist has observed that "it is more difficult to close an unwanted NHS hospital than an unneeded American military base" (Enthoven, 1985). Consultants (senior hospital doctors) with lifetime positions in hospitals had little incentive to run a service more efficiently.[9] There was little incentive to use buildings economically as they had always been paid for by the government. More generally, although comparative data for current hospital costs had been published since the early 1950s and speciality costings had been available since 1988, reliable per unit capital costs were generally absent. More important, there was little incentive for managers to act on the results prior to setting up of the "internal" market in 1991 or to identify more efficient ways of using resources. The flexibility of work practices and pay was limited by national pay settlements. Furthermore, patients could not choose other providers of specialist services even if they were dissatisfied.

The reforms

The motivation for the reforms centred on the belief that an alternative system could be devised that retained the advantages of the NHS – universal coverage and effective cost control – while expanding consumer choice and reducing supply-side inefficiencies. With the reforms, the government aimed to preserve free, or almost free, access to health care and to keep tax-based finance, but to use competition between providers of both hospital and clinical services to improve health and increase consumer satisfaction within a tight budget. In short, it wanted to squeeze more out of the system.

The reforms, which were proposed in a 1989 White Paper (UK DoH, 1989a) and implemented in 1991, did not alter the financial underpinnings of the NHS. The central idea that underpins the new NHS is the distinction between the purchaser and the provider of hospital and community health services (that is, of specialist services usually provided by hospitals). The providers compete with one another to provide such services by means of contracts with purchasers of health services.

Under the new system, there are two kinds of purchaser, each embodying a different model of purchasing. First and largest are the district health authorities (DHAs). The reforms recast their role from one of organising and providing hospital care to selecting the services required to meet those needs and then contracting with various service providers. A greater role than formerly is attached to identifying the health needs of the district's population. Regional health authorities are funded on a formula basis by the central government and in turn allocate resources to DHAs. DHAs are monopsonists in

13

contracting for many hospital services (such as emergency services and other care not contracted for by GP fundholders; see below).

The second type of purchaser is the general practitioner fundholder. GP fundholders are self-employed primary care doctors who manage a budget which they must use to secure a defined range of hospital and primary care services for their patients. The fundholder's practice receives a transfer of roughly one-fifth of the per capita costs of hospital and community health services (such funds previously went directly to the local health authority). With this the fundholder is able to purchase a variety of services and products, including some surgical treatments, diagnoses, prescriptions and, more recently, community nursing services.[10]

GPs must have practices of more than 7 000 (9 000 up to FY 1992/93) patients in order to be eligible to become fundholders. Despite the voluntary nature of the decision to become a fundholder, the take-up by GPs has been quite rapid, especially in rural and suburban areas. About 26 per cent of the population were covered by such purchasers in 1993, a figure which rose to a third in 1994. Since GP fundholders "compete" with DHAs and private insurers in purchasing certain services (with the areas of competition being defined by health care regulation), the purchasing side of market is now also subject to some competitive pressures.[11]

The GP fundholders have considerable flexibility in managing their practice budgets in order to improve the quality of care and to attract more patients. First, they can influence secondary providers' behaviour and improve the quality of services for their patients. Second, they can use surpluses (which are separate from GPs' personal incomes) to purchase further secondary care services or to expand the range of services they provide at their surgeries. Apart from purely professional motivations, GP fundholders have strong pecuniary incentives to make good use of this flexibility – by improving the quality and range of services offered, they are able to attract more patients to their practice, raising their capitation income.[12] GP fundholders can further increase their incomes by using budget surpluses to employ staff to undertake income generating activities, such as immunisations and health promotion.

On the provider side, the reforms centre on the creation of "trust" status for hospitals and on the obligation for all hospitals and community services, regardless of their status, to compete with each other (and in some cases even with private hospitals) for contracts with health authorities, GP fundholders and private insurers in order to earn their income. The trusts are public sector organisations enjoying a high degree of autonomy in providing secondary and community health care. When a hospital or other provider becomes a trust, its assets are transferred to the trustees. The trusts have their own governing body, but are accountable to the NHS management executive, which monitors their financial performance and business plans. Trusts are expected to break even with a required return on assets of 6 per cent. They may employ their staff on their own contracts and terms of service. Trusts may retain unplanned surpluses and are free to borrow within the external financing limit (EFL), which is a form of cash limit set by the Treasury on total borrowing for the sector as a whole. By the end of 1994 well over 90 per cent of hospitals had become trusts.

Other changes introduced as part of the reforms were aimed at ensuring that health service managers were no longer able to view capital expenditure as a "free good". The previous lack of any incentive structure in the management of the NHS estate had led to under-use and neglect of valuable capital assets. The capital charging system was designed to rectify these problems and to encourage managers to make the most efficient use of their physical resources by recognising that the continuing use of those resources has a cost. The capital charging system is now a major input into business planning and ensure that the revenue affordability of any capital investment is carefully considered in respect of its likely impact on contract prices.

The reforms opened up possibilities to overcome some of the weaknesses of the old NHS. Districts and fundholding GPs can, in principle, exercise the sanction of exit against secondary care providers on behalf of consumers. Trusts have the freedom to employ staff at privately contracted wages and conditions. They and non-trust hospitals will have to pay for their use of capital equipment. The Treasury, however, continues to limit overall public sector borrowing for capital spending for the sector as a whole. Trusts can obtain some additional financing of an equity nature under "the private finance initiative" which allows ventures to be undertaken with private sector partners. There will be no free entry to this sector except by private hospitals (which, for the time being, are a small[13] and largely a separate part of the UK health care system).

Changes since the reforms

The government has not established a comprehensive research programme for evaluating the reforms. The discussion below draws on the available research[14] and on various indicators published by the government. However, information remains partial in many areas and it is as yet difficult to take an overall view. The evidence is discussed under several headings: health spending, information, choice, quality of care and equity. The section then turns to a discussion of the response to the reforms of key actors, *i.e.* DHAs, GPs and hospital trusts.

Health spending, activity and efficiency

As noted above, the 1991 changes were intended to improve incentives for efficiency and effectiveness so that the quality of patient care is maximised within whatever resources could be afforded. The changes have, in fact, required higher spending. Contracts, rather than vague understandings, require negotiation before the contract is set and monitoring of compliance after. They require information, especially reliable financial information, something which was not produced under the previous system. Many more managers and financial, accounting and contract staff had to be employed. The result was to increase the budget taken by the NHS in the years before and immediately after the reforms were introduced. Indeed, for a period, the NHS budget rose at rates not seen since the 1960s (see Table 1.4, and Bloor and Maynard, 1993). The government viewed the increases which accompanied the introduction of the new system, at least partly, as an upfront investment to maintain and improve the NHS's efficiency record. An indicator of efficiency gain has been derived by comparing increases in spending on hospitals and community health services (after adjusting for demography and relative prices) with a global indicator of increases in activity.[15] Diagram 1.2 shows that, on this basis, there was an increase in efficiency in the health care sector of about 1.2 per cent per annum between FY 1980/81 and FY 1990/91 – though the rate was declining towards the end of this period. Since the reforms, the annual rate of efficiency gain has increased: to 1.9 per cent in FY 1992/93 with a provisional estimate of 3 per cent in FY 1993/94. The authorities have set a target of least 2¹/₄ per cent in FY 1994/95. In a recent public announcement (HM Treasury, 1993) health spending is slated to be brought back to the low rates of increase seen in the 1980s.

Table 1.4. **National health expenditure control totals**

	Real expenditure (£ billion)	Increase percentage on previous year
1988/89 Pre reform	23.6	–
1989/90 White Paper	23.9	1.3
1990/91 Preparation year	24.9	4.2
1991/92 First year	26.6	6.8
1992/93 Second year	28.3	6.4
1993/94 Third year estimate	29.1	2.8
1994/95 Fourth year plan	29.5	1.4
1995/96 Fifth year plan	29.6	–

Source: H.M. Treasury.

Associated with the increase in efficiency has been a surge in hospital activity although this – and possibly part of the efficiency gains as well – are not independent of the increase in funding. Total hospital inpatients are estimated to have increased at an annual average growth of 5.1 per cent in the three years since FY 1990/91. In the previous seven years the annual rate of growth was only 2.8 per cent. The reforms have given both purchasers and providers new incentives to substitute day surgery for ordinary admission and there has been a sharp rise in day cases. In the three years to FY 1993/94, day cases rose by 16 per cent per annum, a rate more than double that achieved in the seven years before the reforms.

15

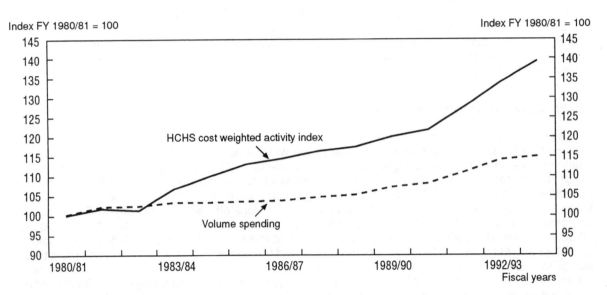

Diagram 1.2. **Hospital and community health services:
Cost-weighted activity index and volume spending[1]**

Index FY 1980/81 = 100

Index FY 1980/81 = 100

HCHS cost weighted activity index

Volume spending

Fiscal years

1. The cost weighted activity index (CWAI) is a measure of the overall increase in activity in Hospital and Community Health Services (HCHS). It is a weighted average of increases in the main areas of HCHS activity using relative contributions to total cost as weights. Volume spending is defined as HCHS cash spending adjusted for changes in HCHS specific pay and price input costs.

Source: UK Department of Health.

Information on costs and outcomes

The reforms have highlighted the need for improved information and mechanisms to produce it are being put in place. This will inevitably be a slow process. Information on both costs and quality of service is still weak even though: the NHS has produced information on current costs at speciality level since 1988; all clinical work is being fully costed, most of it at below speciality level since the introduction of the internal market; and all GP fundholders and extra contractual referral clinical work is costed by episode of care. Although guidelines for costing were issued when the internal market was created, improvements in costing methodology and clinical consistency are being sought and will be introduced over the next three years.[16]

Choice

One of the White Paper's stated intentions for the reforms was to increase patient choice. Patients now have greater freedom to change their GP. In the past, administrative hurdles discouraged patients from changing their doctor. These hurdles have been abolished. Choice remains limited in many rural areas where the density of doctors tends to be low.

A survey has been undertaken comparing the extent to which patients' choice increased in the case of elective surgery referrals in five hospitals in the North West of England (Mahon *et al.*, 1994). The authors conclude that the level of patient involvement was low in 1991 and remained low in the first year of the reforms. Only one in ten patients reported being given a choice of hospital. Only one in twenty patients had been offered any choice of consultant. Two-thirds did not know to whom they were being referred, although this did not, in fact, seem important to people. Nine out of ten patients said they were happy with the way the choice was made.

From the patient's perspective, then, the reforms do not yet appear to have expanded consumer choice significantly. While information is scant, patients of fundholders do not appear to have noticed any increase in alternatives presented to them.

GPs' views of how the reforms have affected their choices are somewhat mixed. Three-quarters of all GPs thought that the reforms had made no difference to the choices available, 17 per cent thought it had made things worse and only 5 per cent thought there had been an improvement. Fundholding GPs, on the other hand, appeared to be more sensitive to the range of choice available. They were more likely to believe there was a viable choice of hospital for their patients and more thought that such factors as waiting times were important for their patients (Mahon et al., 1994).

Quality of care

As yet, there has been no broad-based effort to study the impact of the reforms on the quality of care. One study of elderly people discharged from hospital in 1990 and 1992 (Jones et al., 1994) found little significant improvement in the quality of non-clinical hospital services. In this study it was found that patients waited longer for treatment, on average, in 1992 than in 1990 (even though there was progress made nationally during some of this period). Fewer received information about their hospitals before admission. There were no improvements in food quality or in hospital cleanliness. On the other hand, there were signs that ward staff were trying to improve communication and there was some improvement in the notice patients were given of admission. Ironically though, patient dissatisfaction on this score rose, illustrating a central dilemma for the service: expectations by users are rising all the time, ahead of resources.

Almost no research has been undertaken on trusts so it is difficult to see whether the trust status as such is making any difference to the quality or effectiveness of health care. There is much anecdotal and some survey evidence that individual trusts are making use of their freedom to innovate and improve services. In 1992, a survey of eight trusts covered 900 patients who visited the hospitals before and after they became trusts: 48 per cent said services had improved, 44 per cent said there had been no change and 8 per cent said they had deteriorated (UK DoH, 1993a).

Since the reforms waiting lists have grown but the average waiting time has declined (for those having to wait at all) from an average of 7.6 months in April 1991 to 4.8 months in December 1993.[17] In-patient waiting lists remained fairly stable over the 1980s, falling in the first years of the decade, then rising and stabilising at about 700 000 from the mid-1980s onwards (Bloor and Maynard, 1993). From 1987, day cases were included in the figures. In September 1987 the total number of cases on the waiting lists in England was 848 000. By September 1993 the figure was 1 030 000. Much of the increase was in day cases.

As part of a "Patient's Charter" the Government has pledged that no one should wait more than two years for inpatient or day care and no one should wait more than 18 months for a hip or knee replacement or for a cataract operation.[18] A central waiting fund was established in 1987 and £250 million used to help reduce waiting times. By March 1993, all regions had eliminated waits of over two years. Waits of over a year had also fallen. Whether this constitutes the best use of money is debatable: targeting the neediest cases on the waiting lists rather than reducing overall average waiting times might be a better approach (Gudex et al., 1990).

Recent national attitudes surveys (Social and Community Planning Research, 1994) suggest some increase in satisfaction with the way in which the NHS is run, both among recent users of the service and among the population as a whole. The same surveys also point to a decline in public dissatisfaction with particular aspects of NHS hospital services since the late 1980s.

The reforms encouraged other measures – for example, the medical audit – to help doctors improve their own standards of care through systematic peer review procedures. A study shows that clinicians did respond quite rapidly (Kerrison et al., 1994). The audit process that was studied, however, involved consultants and their juniors and rarely any other professional group. The main method used was a retrospective look at case notes and there was very little consideration of cost, health gain or consumer satisfaction. These weaknesses are now being addressed. An independent evaluation of the audit programme has been established and a high profile national committee, the Clinical Outcomes Group, has been set up to advise on fuller development of clinical audits.

Equity

Though not explicitly stated as a goal in the government's White Paper, equity and equal access are deep in the public's perception of what the NHS is there to deliver. In the past forty odd years since the service was created, it has succeeded in reducing the inequalities in the distribution of GPs and hospital resources between regions. Regional differences in ages at death have declined steadily, at least until the mid-1980s (Whitehead, 1988; Townsend, 1990; Klein, 1991; LeGrand et al., 1990). The North-South divide in mortality has disappeared over the last fifty years for younger age groups, though it remains for older ones (LeGrand and Illsley, 1991). Will the 1991 changes reverse this pattern of improvement?

The United Kingdom has had one of the most sophisticated and effective means of allocating health resources to areas of need. This is a complex area with important lessons for other OECD countries. From 1976 to 1991 allocation of the health budget to regions was based on a formula – actually different formulae for England and Wales, Scotland and Northern Ireland – which reflected the different needs or health status of the population treated in those areas. Under the reforms, the allocation formula was revised. The new regional formula is age-weighted (as was the previous one) but contains lower weight on mortality rates. However, some regions have kept the previous weight on mortality and some have introduced allowances for social deprivation into their formulae for districts. What was arguably more important, was that after the reforms, allocations were made from regions to districts (now purchasers) for their resident populations rather than for the hospitals they contained. The new formula suggests that parts of the south east of England (a relatively prosperous region, but containing areas with elderly populations) need more resources, relative to areas which on other criteria appear to be more deprived. The basis for drawing up the national formula is now being reviewed once again using new data on morbidity from the national population census. The abolition of regions (from April 1996) makes it likely that any new formula will be applied directly to districts.

One of the most persistent concerns has been that the existence of GP fundholders as a separate (and more effective) group of purchasers is creating a two-tier service in terms of the quality of care. During the initial stages of the reform, it was the large and well organised practices in suburban and rural areas that first took advantage of the scheme. As the spread of fundholding progresses these differentials may widen because the quality of service received by those registered with fundholding GPs has improved; the very success of fundholders as purchasers may widen the gap between the quality of services received by their patients and that received by others. It must be emphasised, though, that wide variations in the standard of general practice already existed in the pre-reform national health service. The answer to the potential inequity is not to abandon this effective form of purchasing but to extend fundholding and GP-based purchasing to cover more patients and this is happening.

Response of key actors

DHAs as purchasers

At the outset, in 1991, most hospitals remained "district managed units", but nearly all hospitals will have trust status by the end of 1994. The reforms seem to have clarified DHAs' role as purchasers and to have freed them from having to manage such day-to-day problems as nurse grading reviews, labour disputes and detailed purchasing requirements. It has left hospitals and other providers with a clear mandate to manage themselves. It has also focused districts' attention on thinking about local health needs and priorities (Klein and Redmayne, 1992).

For a number of reasons, however, the split between purchasing and providing services – that is, between the DHAs and the local hospitals – is not yet always very sharp and the districts' purchasing function remains underdeveloped. First, in many districts, a single dominant provider traditionally maintains close links with the DHA and its officials.[19] This may weaken competitive pressures in local health care markets. The long-term possibilities of competition should not be dismissed, however. One study of contracting in the West Midlands, the largest region in the country (Appleby et al., 1994) concluded that about a quarter of the hospitals were in a pure monopoly situation, but that others did face a potentially competitive situation. Second, district officials tend to avoid the political embarrassment likely to follow from decisions not to contract on a large scale with the local hospital. Third, many districts have continued to rely heavily on providers in hospitals to tell them what is needed.[20] Contracting skills are at a premium in the DHAs and the detailed medical knowledge required to bargain on equal terms with a hospital consultant in his or her specialty is often absent. Those in charge of contracting are often inexperienced and poorly equipped to do the job.

General practitioners as purchasers

The aim of the GP fundholding scheme was to give "GPs an opportunity to improve the quality of services on offer to patients, to stimulate hospitals to be more responsive to the needs of GPs and their patients and to develop their own practices for the benefit of their patients".[21] Within the range of services that they are permitted to purchase, GPs do seem to have done a better job of purchasing than DHAs. GP fundholders have been more prepared to diversify providers, to challenge hospital practices and to demand improvements. GPs are closer to patients than DHAs and hear more about their complaints. GPs have the medical knowledge and status needed to confront hospital doctors in contracting. In short, with GPs as purchasers, the information balance is better, though still far from equal. They also have the motivation to contract on patients' behalf (Glennerster *et al.*, 1994). There is considerable logic to more GP-based purchasing (Audit Commission, 1993).

On the other hand, GPs do suffer from a number of competitive disadvantages compared to DHAs. They are less well informed about broader public health questions, such as where to place accident and emergency centres in order to minimise the response time to motor accidents. Since they are small relative to DHAs, transactions costs may be higher for some types of contracting. The optimal boundary between purchasing activities that are solely the responsibility of the DHAs and those in which GP fundholders are allowed to compete is still being tested.

One part of the reforms clearly has begun to show concrete results. GP fundholders are given a cash-limited sum to spend on the drugs they prescribed (in addition to the budget for purchasing hospital care described above). If the GP spends less than this amount the surplus can be used for other treatment. This direct incentive, which applies only to fundholders, has not significantly reduced the cost of prescribing, but it has slowed the rate of increase in fundholders' costs compared to non-fundholders. This is true nationally and in two control trials of fundholders and non-fundholders (Bradlow and Coulter, 1993; Maxwell *et al.*, 1993). The fundholding GPs look more carefully at new and costly drugs and tend to use more generics.[22] In FY 1992/93, the national increase in prescribing costs was 12 per cent but the fundholders' increase was only 8 per cent.

Hospitals and trusts as providers

The new organisational arrangements – trust status and contracting between purchasers and providers – were expected to lead to better performance through devolution of management and through the sharper incentives provided by competition. Initial indications regarding performance of trusts are encouraging. Most trusts have adhered to financial requirements. Trusts have out-performed other hospitals in terms of increases in the number of patients treated. They have been more successful than other hospitals in reducing the number of patients awaiting treatment for more than one year. These performance comparisons are highly inconclusive, however. Hospitals that opted for trust status in the first, and even in the second, year were not a representative sample of UK hospitals. A study by LeGrand and Bartlett (1994) shows that the first hospitals gaining trust status were already the most effective.

In looking at the performance of the new secondary care system, it is necessary to keep in mind the structural context in which these reforms have been implemented. First, the pre-reform NHS was characterised by excess hospital capacity in certain areas[23] and, despite the already-cited downward trend in hospital beds, it remains a problem. Second, with capital costs so much higher, the competitive position of hospitals has been undermined relative to that of doctors' offices and community clinics for treatments that can now be done on an outpatient or day-patient basis. Thus, it is important to assess the impact of reforms by asking whether or not they have enhanced the sectors' capacity to cope with these structural challenges. In this respect, the reforms – by at least opening the door to more flexible financing arrangements and to alliances with other health care actors – almost certainly have been a success, although it is doubtful that they have gone far enough (see below).

Looking ahead

Experience in other areas of policy suggests that shifting from "command and control" to "market-based" systems is not straightforward. In UK health care, the responses of various actors – especially the performance of the GP fundholders – were not entirely anticipated at the time the reforms were enacted. Given the complexity of the sector, unanticipated responses are not unusual, and there will no doubt be further surprises as the market for health services develops over time. By 1996 there will be 80 to 90 DHA purchasers and possibly 15 000 GP fundholders in groups of purchasing consortia. On the supplier side, 450 trusts (possibly fewer, taking into account closures and amalgamation) are expected in 1996. Within this general context policy makers must continue refining a policy strategy that will discipline spending pressures, maximise efficiency and welfare gains and allow structural change to occur – permitting successful innovations and institutions to take hold and unsuccessful experiments to be eliminated. In the nearer term, a number of specific problems need to be addressed if the reforms are to have their full positive impacts. These are taken up in the following paragraphs.

Structural adjustment in the hospital sector

As a result of political and technological developments, pressures for change are likely to be particularly intense for hospitals. Up to the present, competition has been very limited: contracts have been set to maintain the *status quo* and purchasers have been instructed to give considerable warning of their intention to take their custom elsewhere. But as competition increases and some hospitals prove more attractive providers than others, some will wish to expand as others contract or close. Rules for exit have not yet been clearly established. Pressures are already appearing in high cost urban areas, particularly in London. The government has stated its intention to reduce beds in inner cities but there is considerable opposition from local interest groups particularly in the London area. In this context, the government had set up the London Implementation Group to find appropriate solutions which go with the grain of the market. The decisions should help set the criteria and rules which can guide the development of the market in the future. More generally, the government needs to make it clear that market signals must be heeded if appropriate resource reallocation decisions are to take place.

Hospitals will undoubtedly follow several strategies in responding to structural pressures. Hospital amalgamation, particularly if economies of scale and scope obtain, may be one way to proceed to reduce excess capacity and this is being tried in London. Vertical integration may be an option for hospitals wishing to provide a broader package of services – such as nursing and primary care as well as acute care. At the other extreme, hospitals may find cost savings from increased specialisation in certain areas and – given that patient risks from surgery tend to be lower in hospitals where there are high volumes – there may be strong medical grounds for this. It is not yet clear that the current administrative framework for determining entry, exit, expansion and contraction in the hospital sector will be able to cope with upcoming adjustment challenges. It therefore becomes increasingly important to clarify the ground-rules for such processes in the sector.

Unlike the areas around major cities and in the densely populated south-east of England, some regions may not have large enough patient volumes to support several large hospitals. Indeed, one of the main adjustment challenges for health care policy will be to encourage a service structure that allows such areas to be served in a cost-effective manner. In these circumstances, care should be taken to avoid closing down hospitals without first giving them a chance to explore various survival strategies (*e.g.* through vertical integration). For this to happen, trusts may need to run losses over the short term, something they are not currently allowed to do. Allowing trusts to borrow on private markets may also be an option as long as it is clear that there is no obligation by the government to bail them out. In some sparsely populated areas, though, the market may not be able to support more than one hospital (meaning that it is, in essence, a local natural monopoly). Here, other regulatory mechanisms for pricing may need to be envisaged (similar to those used for public utilities).

Further decentralisation of decision making

In principle, hospital trusts have been given the freedom to manage and to negotiate separate agreements with their employees. In practice, this has been curtailed. The central authorities have been reluctant to permit full decentralisation and have intervened over pay and in a number of operational matters. Ministers have now expressed the clear intention that local pay bargaining should take effect in the coming year's wage round. This process needs to be extended further. Without a clearer separation of roles and a substantial increase in operating freedom, the trusts cannot be expected to produce the hoped-for efficiency gains.

At the same time, trusts will need to tighten control over their own resources. Most have had to take over existing contractual arrangements for labour and very few have tried to modify these in any significant way and then only for new staff.[24] Integrating clinicians – who are key to the production process – into the management of hospitals, has a considerable way to go, even though this was a requirement for obtaining trust status. Wages of hospital doctors are still largely determined centrally and the attribution of distinction awards (which accord large wage increases and form a key role in doctor incentives) is still partly centralised and heavily influenced by the clinicians themselves although there is increasing input from local management. Making the medical staff more accountable for achieving overall goals of the hospital, with the ability to sanction where necessary, is likely to be a key element in achieving efficiency gains.

Some hospitals may wish to invest either to improve the quality of services provided or, where they have proved successful in attracting business, to expand. As it stands, trust hospitals can retain surpluses earned and some narrow scope exists to re-invest them. In addition, there is an overall External Financing Limit for total borrowing for capital expenditure established by the Treasury. The rules for attributing capital, while requiring certain rate of return criteria to be achieved, are still based on administrative rules rather than on market criteria. Hospitals have only limited scope to borrow in private markets, although private equity investment in collaborative arrangements with the private sector is being encouraged under the Private Finance Initiative. Rules in this area may also need to be examined.

Improved pricing practices

Correcting the weakness of the DHAs' contracting capability will require the progressive "unbundling" of contracts in order to permit better comparison of the cost of particular services between hospitals and better monitoring of contracts. This, in turn, means that providers must enhance transparency through better cost accounting and information on outputs so that contract performance can be monitored and evaluated. At the same time greater discretion must be given to hospitals in setting prices. Under current arrangements, hospitals must set prices in line with average costs to ensure that total costs are covered. However, this reduces the scope for competition on the basis of marginal cost pricing as well as for innovation and downward pressures on costs. Hence, it is not surprising that little competition on price has taken place outside of the London area.

Better purchasing co-ordination and better information

The White Paper "The Health of the Nation" (1991) presented the government's health strategy and objectives.[25] It set targets in selected areas and stressed the importance of prevention in achieving them. These goals are to be reflected in the NHS strategies in purchasing health care and other health-related services at the regional and district level. The White Paper proposes an extensive system of consultation and co-ordination to achieve coherent policies affecting health. In its aims, the government would appear to be in the forefront of countries attempting to achieve more coherent health policies which recognise that health care is only one part – albeit an important one – in improving health. The purchaser-provider split provides a means of re-orienting funds towards prevention if this is demonstrated to be more cost effective.

Nonetheless, the government's approach – taken in the context of the NHS reforms – is likely to run up against some difficulties. First, information on the effectiveness of preventive measures is weak, although this problem is not limited to the United Kingdom alone. Much more information is required here. The current GP contract, which now stipulates a number of core services to be provided and financial incentives for a number of preventive measures, is a case in point. For some of these measures, there is little evidence as to whether the financial incentives are cost effective and whether the financial rewards are in line with the expected benefits, although this is critical in establishing more appropriate incentive structures (Scott and Maynard, 1991).

Second, the incentives set up by the current payment arrangements need to be monitored. It is often not easy to recognise poorly structured incentives until the sector has had time to fully adjust to them. The potential problems here are cost shifting, under-serving and "cream skimming". In the case of fundholders, these incentives appear to have been reduced since the budget resources they receive are entirely separate from their practice income.[26] On the other hand, hospitals may attempt to shift some of the cost onto community service budgets of local authorities (home help and residential care), for example, by discharging patients early.

Improved contracting

Intensifying competition in health care crucially depends on the capacity of the DHAs to contract effectively. With a few exceptions, this has been the weakest area of the reforms. GP fundholders proved initially more adept in this area, partly reflecting the fact that their medical knowledge serves to balance the power of hospital specialists. For the DHAs, block contracts were the norm at the beginning as the government attempted to ease in the reforms by maintaining the *status quo*. Since then, DHAs have become progressively more adept and contracts have evolved although at differing speeds across DHAs. There is evidence of shifts in spending taking place and DHAs are increasingly looking to market test services. Improving the purchasing function in the new internal market is a stated key priority of the government (UK DoH, 1993b; NHSME, 1993). Since long-standing relationships are likely to be sustained between purchasers and providers for much of secondary care – such as emergency services – the risk of "cosy" relationships continuing or becoming re-established will remain strong.

Here again, though, an important problem facing DHAs is the lack of information. In the past medical priorities were largely determined by the medical corps. More needs to be known about the health needs of the population. While important progress has been made in developing an agreed set of population health outcome measure,[27] further work needs to be done to establish where health care can make the greatest contribution to health status. Likewise, not enough is known about the costs of individual components of health care, so that costs can be balanced against expected gains. Finally, information on the quality and quantity of output provided is often wanting, making monitoring of contracts more difficult. Purchasers will also need to progress further in the evaluation of the appropriateness of the health care provided, ensuring, for example, that it is in line with accepted protocols. This may require increasing the medical expertise within the purchasing agencies themselves. This capacity for evaluation needs to be extended to the general practitioners as well.

Longer-term considerations

It is not yet clear how the new arrangements will affect the long-run development in areas such as medical research and development; human capital accumulation in the sector; and the organisational arrangements by which the various actors – government, teaching and research institutions, service providers and purchasers – co-ordinate these various activities. If the goal of improving information on the effectiveness and cost of different treatments is realised, this will ultimately provide clearer signals for much of the long-term development of the sector. But at the same time, local purchasing practices, which attempt to get best value for money, will gradually erode the possibilities of financing research, teaching and training through cross-subsidisation within hospitals. This may require establishing greater central financing and control specifically aimed at supporting these functions.

Concluding remarks

Reforms of the UK national health service, implemented since 1991, are a bold attempt to introduce elements of competition into the centrally-financed health care system which has succeeded in delivering adequate services to all citizens at reasonable overall cost to the economy. Reaching any overall conclusion about the impact of the reforms on the Health Service is premature. The main elements, the separation of purchaser and provider, and the creation of hospital trusts and fundholding general practitioners (GPs), are taking effect only gradually. The contracting capacity and the information to do it well are being acquired only slowly. There are costs to contracting and to monitoring. There has been little systematic research on the impact of the changes, something to which the government had paid little attention until recently. What research there is gives increasingly encouraging results. Fundholders and hospital trusts appear to be contracting mainly with the same providers as before rather than effecting major changes in supply arrangements. Nevertheless, in a market as large and complex as that of health services, structural changes may realistically be expected to occur first only at the margins of traditional arrangements, and such changes do indeed appear to be happening. For example, the competitive element introduced, especially by fundholders, does appear to be making hospitals to respond to patients' needs and to improve efficiency. There are also indications that needs-based purchasing, rather than block contracts, is providing a clearer role for purchasing agencies. How to divide the purchasing functions between fundholding GPs and district health authorities, and how to link these to general goals for health outcomes are issues which are now being addressed in a variety of ways. Similarly the regulatory framework within which this "market" will develop has yet to be spelled out clearly, particularly as regards to exit, entry and structural adjustment in the hospital sector. But, these issues are under active consideration.

A key to success in transforming a command-and-control system into a more flexible and efficient one is to give competitive forces the chance and time to work themselves out fully before intervening to deal with any apparent market failures to produce desirable outcomes. The criticism that improved quality of services provided through GP fundholders is creating a two-tier system is a case in point. There has always been an element of inequity because the competence of GPs as well as the circumstances in which they practise differ substantially. There is no firm evidence that inequity has risen with the emergence of GP fundholders. If there were to be any transitory rise in inequity of this kind, it should be tolerated, as it would largely reflect efficiency gains. The answer should be sought by "levelling-up" – by expanding the number of fundholding GPs – rather than regulating them. Another case is closure of hospitals in large cities, which are experiencing financial difficulties because they are losing patients as a result of reforms. While it is understandable that political solutions are being sought for such sensitive issues, it is important that solutions go in the direction of facilitating, rather than retarding, adjustment and that the ways in which the downsizing takes place be guided by market signals. More generally, it will be imperative that the hospital trusts make use of their new freedoms to invest (including those offered by the private finance initiative) or divest, as well as exercising fully the freedom already given to them in terms of personnel policies and capital allocation. To be able to deliver better performance, trusts need to respond to sharper incentives than hitherto.

Notes

1. Community health services cover a range of health-related service of a non-acute nature such as home nursing and care for the frail elderly.

2. That is, deaths from all causes (except suicides) between ages 0 and 64, weighted in each case by the number of years until age 65 which would have been reached.

3. In the case of life expectancy at age 60 (which, compared with other health outcome indicators, has a relatively high correlation with health expenditure per capita in OECD countries), the United Kingdom does not appear to do as well. The United Kingdom is at over one standard error below its "predicted" level based on a simple cross-section regression between the life expectancy and health spending variables.

4. More generally, these comparisons of volume growth should be treated with care as health prices are partly derived from accounting procedures for the public services that differ between countries.

5. Many studies have found that differences in GDP (or Total Domestic Expenditure) per capita are the most significant "predictors" of inter-country differences in per capita health spending (e.g. Newhouse, 1977; Gerdtham, 1991). The causal mechanisms, if any, behind this relationship are not clear, however, and care is therefore required in drawing conclusions or policy inferences from the relationship. In almost all cases, the level or resources to be devoted to health care stems from collective rather than individual decisions. GDP per capita may be a proxy for a variety of factors, related more or less to income and economic well-being (possibly including the size of public budgets), which influence these health spending decisions.

6. For example, capitation rather than fee for service payment arrangements for doctors and a significant share of public spending in total health care. See Gerdtham (1991) for further analysis.

7. As has been pointed out in previous reviews of the health care sector, expenditure or budgetary control is often a problem in both publicly-and privately-managed insurance schemes. The French health care system (OECD, 1994) relies heavily on a reimbursement plan run by public insurers with private fee-for-service delivery of ambulatory services. The United States' quite diverse health care system – featuring large numbers of public and private insurers who reimburse fee-for service providers – is also characterised by extremely rapid expenditure growth (OECD, 1992a). Both reviews emphasise the need for an enforceable health budget constraint backed up by measures that allow purchasers of health services to contract for delivery of a prespecified bundle of services at a competitively-determined price.

8. See OECD (1992b, p. 73) and OECD (1991/1992, p. 56). Both analyses point more or less explicitly to public health systems that cannot compete effectively with private health services even though the public health service charges close to zero prices.

9. In fact, incentives may have been perverse in some cases. Where consultants had private practices in addition to their positions in hospitals, there was a potential conflict of interest. The consultant could offer to serve a patient through his private practice after informing the patient that, in order to obtain the same service through the NHS, he would have to spend a considerable time on the waiting list in the public sector.

10. Fundholders are accountable to the NHS Management Executive through regional health authorities. These frequently delegate day-to-day management of fundholders to the Family Health Service Authorities (FHSAs) who also have responsibility for administering the family doctor services provided by all GPs.

11. These pressures are limited by a number of factors. First, there are few GP fundholders in some districts; in these districts, then, there is little alternative to DHA purchasing. Another factor that limits competition is the fact that one cannot go to one GP for primary health care and to another for secondary health care purchasing. The two services continue to be "bundled" together. This might weaken competitive pressure in purchasing, especially if switching GPs by patients is costly.

12. This means that there is little direct incentive for under-serving.

13. In some market segments – notably for the frail elderly – private health care provision is important.

14. The King's Fund financed several research projects designed to evaluate the changes. The research results are published in Robinson and LeGrand (1994).

15. The Health Care and Hospital Service activity indicator.

16. The National Health Management Executive is issuing a series of detailed and informative guides to health needs assessments on an area basis using the best epidemiological research and a complementary series of assessments of the cost-effectiveness of health service interventions. A UK Clearing House for Information on the Assessment of Health Outcomes has been set up at the Nuffield Institute in Leeds. This will be a resource centre for work on health outcomes research. Government has also set up a Standing Committee on Health Technology Assessment which is in the process of evaluating treatments, approaches and technical changes in health care.

17. Fifty per cent of admissions are nonetheless immediate.

18. The Patient's Charter – part of a wider strategy which builds on the Government's Citizen's Charter initiative to improve standards in the delivery of public services generally – was brought into effect on 1 April 1992. It sets out the public's right to NHS services and introduced three new rights addressing information, complaints handling, and waiting times for inpatient treatment. The Charter also introduced the concept of standard setting (at national and local level) as a means to improve the quality of service delivery. Further revision is due at the end of 1994 to include more new standards which will strengthen current guarantees/standards for inpatient and outpatient waiting times and include new standards for hospital catering and community nursing appointments.

19. This is the result of the government policy pursued since 1961 to build large district general hospitals to serve most of the needs of the district. District Health Authorities were set up to run them.

20. For two local case studies and a discussion of the issues, see Bartlett and Harrison (1993) and Appleby *et al.* (1994). One evaluation of purchasing in the West Midlands concluded: "Evidence from our project over the last three years suggests that purchasers were still trying to get to grips with the basic information they required to assess health care needs and make rational decisions concerning the choice of provider – based on quantifiable measures of quality, reliable data on prices, and, importantly, local opinion. But in addition, purchasers are only just beginning to grapple with the underlying methodologies of priority setting, the construction of contracts and the information implications of monitoring contract performance" (Appleby *et al.*, 1994, pp. 51-52).

21. See UK DoH (1989*b*).

22. In Oxfordshire, for example, the net cost of ingredients for fundholders in dispensing practices increased by 10 per cent, for non-dispensers by 13 per cent but for non-fundholders by nearly 19 per cent (Bradlow and Coulter, 1993).

23. Excess capacity is a particular problem in London and in other big cities, whose large teaching hospitals had previously attracted patients from all over the country. This was because their specialists had national or international reputations and because the treatment they offered was essentially free to the district from which the patient came (or, to be more accurate, the cross charging was so complex that it did not enter into the decision process). Under the reforms, districts must pay for any patients sent to such hospitals, often much more than would be the case if patients were treated in a local hospital. This is resulting in the loss of custom by long-established teaching hospitals. Faced with the possibility that several famous London teaching hospitals might close, the government quickly removed the issue from the market place and appointed a committee to consider the future of London hospitals and a series of specialty reviews. Some mergers have been announced during 1994, the details of which were still "under consultation" at the time of writing.

24. There have been some changes in a few areas – for example in ambulance trusts where changes in wage scales have followed the move to trust status.

25. The White Paper embodies an illness-related approach to improving the health status of the population and sets targets for desired health outcomes. The targets are grouped in five "key areas" selected on the basis of three criteria:
    - that they represent significant burdens of ill-health and/or premature mortality for the population;
    - that they are areas in which effective interventions may be possible;
    - that monitoring the results and measuring outcomes achieved are possible.

    The initial key areas are coronary heart disease and stroke, cancers, mental illness, HIV/AIDS and sexual health, and accidents.

26. Under capitation, GPs could shift the cost of difficult cases by sending them to hospital specialists. Since they now have to purchase specialist services out of the fundholding budget there is a cost to this behaviour.

27. See UK DoH (1993*c* and 1993*d*).

Bibliography

Appleby, J., P. Smith, W. Ranade, V. Little and R. Robinson (1994), "Monitoring Managed Competition", in Robinson and LeGrand (eds.), *Revaluating the NHS Reforms*, Kings Fund Institute, London.

Audit Commission (1993), *Practices Make Perfect: the Role of the Family Health Services Authority,* HMSO, London.

Barr, N., H. Glennerster and J. Le Grand (1988), "Reform and the NHS", Welfare State Paper No. 32, London School of Economics.

Bartlett, W. and L. Harrison (1993), "Quasi Markets and the National Health Service Reforms", in Le Grand and Bartlett (eds.), *Quasi Markets and Social Policy*, Macmillan, London.

Bloor, K. and A. Maynard (1993), "Expenditure on the NHS During and After the Thatcher Years: its Growth and Utilisation", Discussion Paper 113, Centre for Health Economics, York.

Bradlow, J. and A. Coulter (1993), "Effect of fundholding and indicative prescribing schemes on general practitioners' prescribing costs", *British Medical Journal,* Vol. 307, pp. 1186-1189.

Enthoven, A. (1985), *Reflections on the Management of the NHS,* Nuffield Trust, London.

Gerdtham, Ulf-G. (1991), "Essays on international comparisons of Health Care Expenditure", *Linköping Studies in Art and Science 66,* Linköping, Sweden.

Glennerster, H., M. Matsaganis, P. Owens and S. Hancock (1994), "Wild Card or Winning Hand: GP fundholding", in Robinson and LeGrand, *op. cit.*

Gudex, C., A. Williams, Jourdan *et al.* (1990), "Prioritising Waiting Lists", *Health Trends,* Vol. 2, No. 3, pp. 103-108.

H.M. Treasury (1993), *Financial Statement and Budget Report 1994-95,* HMSO, London.

Jones, D., C. Lester and R. West (1994), "Monitoring Changes in Health Services for Older People", in Robinson and LeGrand, *op. cit.*

Jowell, R. *et al.* (1991), *British Social Attitudes*, 8th Report, Gower, Aldershot.

Kerrison, S., T. Packwood and M. Buxton (1994), "Monitoring Medical Audit", in Robinson and LeGrand, *op. cit.*

Kings Fund Institute (1988), *Health Finance: Assessing the Options,* London.

Klein, R. (1991), "Making sense of inequalities: a response to Peter Townsend", *International Journal of Health Services,* Vol. 21, pp. 175-181.

Klein, R. and S. Redmayne (1992), *Patterns of Priorities: a study of the purchasing and rationing policies of health authorities,* NAHAT, Birmingham.

LeGrand, J. and W. Bartlett (1994), "The Performance of Trusts", in Robinson and LeGrand, *op. cit.*

LeGrand, J. and R. Illsley (1991), "Regional Inequalities in Mortality", LSE Welfare State Discussion Paper, LSE, London.

LeGrand, J., D. Winter and Woolley (1990), "NHS Safe in Whose Hands?", in J. Hills (ed.), *The State of Welfare,* Oxford University Press, Oxford.

Mahon, A., D. Wilkin and C. Whitehouse (1994), "Choice of Hospital for Elective Surgery Referral: GPs and Patients' Views", in Robinson and LeGrand, *op. cit.*

Maxwell, M., D. Heaney, J.G.R. Howie and S. Noble (1993), "General practice fundholding: observations on prescribing patterns and costs using the defined daily dose method", *British Medical Journal,* Vol. 307, pp. 1190-1194.

National Health Service Management Plan (1993), *The National Health Service Management Executive Business Plan 1993/94,* HMSO, London.

Newhouse, J.P. (1977), "Medical care expenditure: a cross national survey", *Journal of Human Resources,* 12, pp. 115-125.

OECD (1991/1992), *Economic Survey of Greece,* p. 56, Paris.

OECD (1992a), *The Reform of Health Care: a Comparative Analysis of Seven Countries,* Paris.

OECD (1992b), *Economic Survey of Italy,* p. 73, Paris.

OECD (1994), *Economic Survey of France*, p. 66, Paris.

Propper, C. and A. Maynard (1990), "Whither the Private Health Care Sector", in A.J. Culyer, A.K. Maynard, and J.W. Posnett (eds.), *Competition in Health Care: Reforming the NHS,* Macmillan, London.

Propper, C. and O'Donnell (1991), "Equity and the Distribution of NHS Resources", *Journal of Health Economics,* Vol. 10, pp. 1-19.

Robinson, R. and J. LeGrand (eds.) (1994), *Evaluating the NHS Reforms,* Kings Fund Institute, London.

Scott, T. and A. Maynard (1991), *Will the New GP Contract Lead to Cost Effective Medical Practice,* University of York, Centre for Health Economics, Discussion Paper No. 82.

Social and Community Planning Research (1994), *British Social Attitudes Survey.*

Taylor-Gooby, P. (1991), "Attachment to the Welfare State", in Jowell, *op. cit.*

Townsend, P. (1990), "Widening Inequalities in Health: a rejoinder to Rudolf Klein", *International Journal of Health Services,* Vol. 20, pp. 363-372.

UK DoH (1989a), *Working for Patients,* Cm 555, HMSO, London.

UK DoH (1989b), *Practice Budgets for General Medical Practitioners*, Working Paper 3, HMSO, London.

UK DoH (1993a), *Government Response to First Report from Health Committee 1992-93*, Cm 2152, HMSO, London.

UK DoH (1993b), *The Government's Expenditure Plans 1993-94 to 1995-96: Departmental Report*, Cm 2212, HMSO, London.

UK DoH (1993c), *Population Health Outcome Indicators for the NHS – a feasibility study*, HMSO, London.

UK DoH (1993d), *Population Health Outcome Indicators for the NHS, 1993 – England – a consultation document*, HMSO, London.

Whitehead, M. (1988), "The health divide", in Townsend, P., Davidson, N. and Whitehead, M. (eds.), *Inequalities in Health*, Penguin, London.

Chapter 2

CANADA

Despite a wide variation in the organisation of health systems within the OECD area, a general trend – with Canada being no exception – has been for health expenditures to account for a growing share of GDP. Among Member countries, Canada ranks second highest in health expenditure per capita behind the United States (with recent data revisions, Switzerland became second and Canada third). However, the two North American health systems are at almost opposite extremes with respect to government intervention. In contrast to the United States, Canadian governments play a major role in the regulation and funding of health-care, suggesting that comparing levels in health expenditure alone is of limited value when assessing the relative costs and benefits of a particular health system. Instead, one must account for the public's desired health-care regime, an area where Canada has specific goals. Canada's objectives of universal and comprehensive health coverage have led to a system where consumers face a zero price for medically necessary services. Nevertheless, increasing claims of quantity rationing and growing concern about the adequacy of the services provided and their resulting benefits suggest that the system may be increasingly falling short of its goals.[1] This raises questions whether a) the principles underlying the Canadian health system are conducive to the efficient delivery of health services, and b) more explicit incentive mechanisms and increased accountability are necessary to achieve the desired goals of the health system while enhancing efficiency.

In an effort to address these issues, this chapter first outlines the main features of the Canadian health system and compares them internationally. The outcomes and costs of the system are then examined, with particular emphasis on the key factors underlying the growth in health expenditure. Policy responses aiming at cost-containment and enhancing efficiency – while minimising infringements on the principles underlying the system – are subsequently described.

Main features of the system

The institutional setting

The Canadian health care system is made up of ten provincial and two territorial public health insurance schemes, each of which is universal and publicly funded. Although differing in detail across provinces, the health schemes are linked through their adherence to national minimum requirements, as mandated in the Canada Health Act (1984).[2] They are defined by five broad principles:

- *Universality*, which requires that 100 per cent of the insured persons of the province must be entitled to the insured health services of the provincial health insurance plan on uniform terms and conditions.
- *Comprehensiveness* in insuring all medically necessary health services.
- *Accessibility* by insured persons to medically necessary health services on uniform terms and conditions and without barriers, including charges to patients for insured health services.
- *Portability* of insured health coverage for insured persons when they move within Canada or travel inside or outside the country.
- *Public administration*, ensuring that the provincial health insurance plan is administered on a non-profit basis by a public authority appointed or designated by the provincial government and subject to audits.

The jurisdiction over health care remains with the provincial governments, with the federal government's role in delivering care services being limited to specific groups – accounting for less than

2 per cent of total public health expenditure.[3] Importantly, the range of health goods and services covered by provincial health plans is defined at the provincial government level. The public health-care system is organised as a mixture of public funding with private provision (see below). Approximately three-quarters of all health care expenditure is public, private expenditure being largely related to dentists and other private-based allied health professionals such as chiropractors and opticians, and outside hospital drugs and appliances (Diagram 2.1). Private sector health provision has grown slowly over the 1980s from 25 to 28 per cent of total health expenditure.[4]

Health care provision consists of predominantly self-employed physicians, and hospitals which are generally non-profit entities guided by community boards of trustees. The majority of physicians operate on a "fee-for-service" basis and submit claims to provincial health insurance plans. Physicians retain the ability to opt-out of the provincial health insurance schemes and bill patients directly, although there are few financial advantages. Patients remain relatively free to choose their primary health-care general practitioner and a limited number of specialists. The physicians, or general practitioners, are considered the "gate-keepers" to the system, since they are the initial point of contact for the public. This enables them to control referrals to specialists and admissions to hospitals, while also determining the need for, and prescription of, any treatment. Most hospitals are owned by either voluntary organisations, municipal or provincial authorities, or to a lesser extent religious orders. Less than 5 per cent of Canada's hospitals are privately owned, with the majority of these operating in long-term care.[5]

Health insurance covers all medically necessary hospital and physician services as well as certain surgical dental procedures, as defined independently in each jurisdiction. Hospital services include in-patient care, drugs, supplies, tests, and some out-patient services. Physician services cover all medically required services available in hospitals, clinics or physicians' offices. The degree of coverage across provinces varies for other services such as drugs,[6] ambulance services, long-term care, dental care, home-care, and optometry. The range and scope of health care services covered by the provincial insurance plans has changed over time, having expanded during the 1970s – albeit at differing rates across provinces – before contracting in more recent years. Private health insurance that duplicates services offered by the public schemes is prohibited, and there are no deductibles or co-payments for medically necessary services.[7]

Diagram 2.1. **Total health expenditure by provider**

Per cent

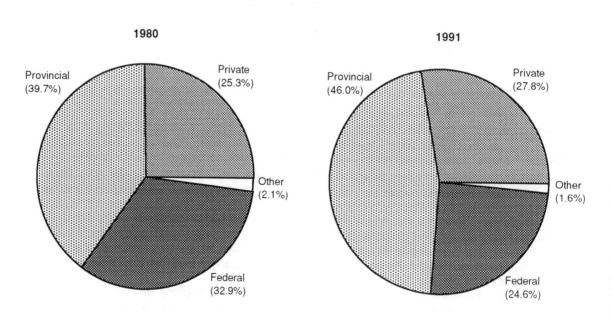

Source: Health and Welfare Canada.

Several factors underlie the government involvement in providing health care, mostly related to issues of equity and market failure. For example, public intervention was judged desirable to minimise the negative externalities of poor health, especially given that insufficient incentives often exist to ensure adequate individual provision of health care. Regulation of the health sector also appeared necessary given the asymmetry of medical expertise and information. The medical profession is both the supplier of care and the agent for deciding "appropriate" consumption levels, leaving little role for the consumer and/or funder. Furthermore, if health care is not to be denied on the basis of an individual's income, some form of public intervention into the health market is warranted. This is especially so given that free-market health insurance can lead to provider and consumer strategies which lower both the efficiency and equity of health care.[8] This "market failure" arises since the health sector is generally non-competitive, instead often characterised by a limited number of non-profit motivated producers, heterogeneous products, ill-informed consumers, and third-party purchasers. In summary, a public health system – with the government acting as a single payer – appears appropriate if both risk-pooling of individuals and a redistribution of wealth from low to high health-risk individuals is desired.

Funding arrangements

The federal-provincial mix

The funding of the health system (Diagram 2.2) is undertaken at both the federal and provincial level of government. Provincial governments receive federal funding according to the Established Programs Financing (EPF) arrangements adopted in 1977 in return for adhering to the five previously mentioned principles set out in the 1984 Canada Health Act. The transfer was escalated annually according to a three-year moving average of GNP increases, equalising the total EPF growth on a per capita basis across provinces. Largely in response to the rising federal deficits, the growth of the escalator was cut by 2 per cent in the 1986 federal budget, and a further 1 per cent in the 1989 budget. The Expenditure Control Plan, introduced in 1990, subsequently froze the growth of per capita entitlements for the 1991-92 years, with this freeze later extended until 1995. The combined effect of this and growing provincial health expenditure, has been an increase in the financial burden on provincial governments.[9]

Provincial funding methods differ across provinces,[10] although they are sourced from general tax revenue. This is favoured due primarily to equity characteristics – as opposed to efficiency concerns[11] – in order to adhere more easily to the principles of the 1984 Health Act. Under the Act, a province is entitled to the full cash portion of its federal transfer payment provided that no user charges or extra billing exists for medically necessary health services, and that none of the five principles of the legislation are contravened.[12] However, the federal government's ability to enforce the Health Act may prove increasingly difficult in the future. This is because the federal transfers are delivered through a combination of both tax points and a cash transfer. It is the cash component of the transfer which is withheld in the case of provincial non-adherence to the Act. However, this is the component which is diminishing as the total EPF transfers are constrained by the federal government.[13]

Physician payments

Throughout most of the 1980s all provinces excluding Quebec (see Annex) financed medical care open-endedly, paying physicians on a "fee-for-service" basis.[14] That is, provincial governments paid all eligible claims submitted by physicians for services rendered at a negotiated fee rate. Physicians fees were set following annual consultation between physician groups and provincial governments. These focused on the overall percentage increase to be applied to an existing schedule, while service utilisation rates remained open ended – implying limited control over total provincial medical care expenditure. Progressively during the 1980s, in response to rising medical service costs, provinces began to implement caps to physician remuneration. These generally took the form of reduced incentives to provide services (for example, services beyond a certain billing limit are offset by a percentage reduction in the fee payment, see below).

Hospital financing

Hospitals, which are almost entirely public or non-profit community facilities, receive their budget as provincial government lump-sum grants. These global budgets are determined through bilateral negoti-

Diagram 2.2. **Funding structure of Canada's health system**

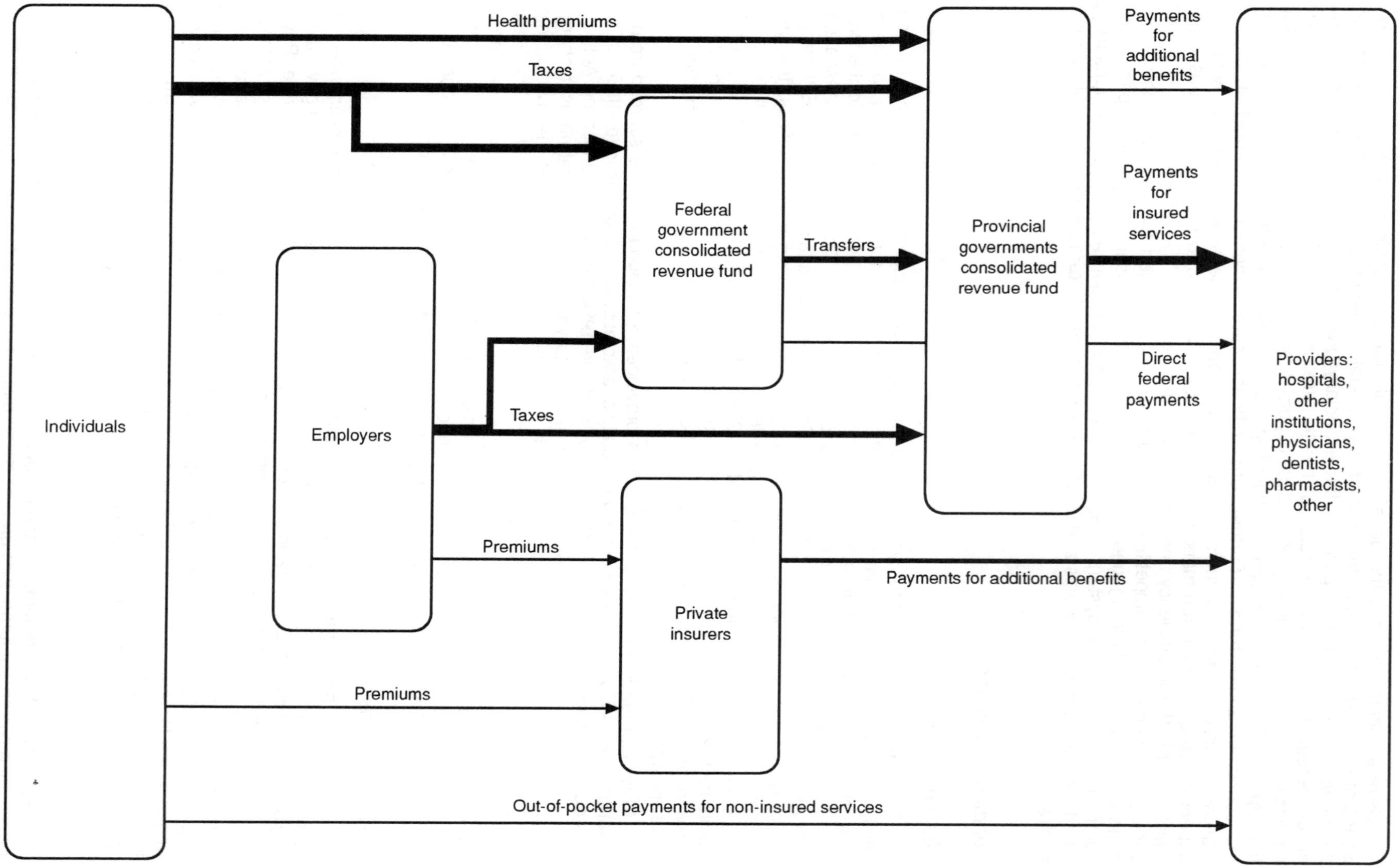

Providers: hospitals, other institutions, physicians, dentists, pharmacists, other

Payments for additional benefits

Payments for insured services

Direct federal payments

Payments for additional benefits

Out-of-pocket payments for non-insured services

Provincial governments consolidated revenue fund

Transfers

Federal government consolidated revenue fund

Private insurers

Health premiums

Taxes

Taxes

Premiums

Premiums

Premiums

Employers

Individuals

ation at the commencement of each financial period, and represent a change from the 1970s line by line budget negotiations. The advantage of this system is that it allows hospital boards to allocate funds within their institution according to local needs and enables more effective planning through improved predictability. Hospital boards may be elected by the entity owning the facility or appointed by a provincial/territorial government. Membership might include: representatives from the general community; doctors, dentists, pharmacists, nurses or other staff of the institution (only in some provinces); the foundation associated with the hospital and the executive officer of the hospital. Provincial governments can also more effectively contain costs through rigid enforcement of budget limits, as has been the trend since the late 1980s. Several factors may be used in the determination of global budgets, including growth in the volume of workloads, average length of hospital stays, total patient days, demographic changes, general price increases, and special programmes.

An important feature of Canada's approach to hospital budgeting is the separation of operating expenses and capital spending. The funding of capital expenditure differs widely across provinces, although the common features include prior approval of the provincial Minister of Health based on a needs assessment, and the compulsory participation of municipal governments and/or privately raised funds (ranging between 10 to 40 per cent). Given that the authority to approve the expenditure is left with the provincial government, who will then have to cover the ongoing operating costs, approval is not given lightly.

International comparison

As briefly described above, the Canadian system of health insurance falls between the extremes of private and nationalised health-care regimes. In a private insurance system (as it exists to some extent in the United States) the government regulates but generally does not fund or provide health care, while in a national health service system (as found in the United Kingdom prior to its 1991 reforms) the government carries out all these three functions. In Canada, the federal and provincial governments are responsible for both regulating and funding, but provide only a small proportion of total health care. In terms of expenditure, the public sector accounts for about three quarters of health care; this is close to the OECD average and compares with about two fifths in the United States and more than four fifths in the United Kingdom.

The way in which health care is provided can significantly affect spending because in-patient care tends to be more expensive than ambulatory care. Countries in which the ambulatory-care and hospital sectors are similar in size in terms of cost (such as Germany and Japan) seem to control their expenditures better. In Canada, the hospital sector is relatively important, with its share of total spending – though declining – more than double that of ambulatory care (Table 2.1). Spending on pharmaceuticals is about average; but while in the OECD area its share of total health expenditure has remained stable it has risen markedly in Canada over the past decade, reflecting strong price increases

Table 2.1. **The structure of expenditure on health**
Share of major components in total expenditure, in per cent

	1980			1990		
	Hospital care	Ambulatory care	Pharmaceuticals	Hospital care[1]	Ambulatory care[2]	Pharmaceuticals
Canada	52.6	22.1	8.9	49.2	21.9	13.3
France	48.1	24.8	15.9	44.2	28.4	16.8
Germany	36.1	26.6	18.7	37.8	28.9	22.0
Italy	54.0	29.5	13.9	49.1	28.8	19.3
Japan	30.7	44.3	22.1	31.1	40.5	17.3
United Kingdom	56.1	..	11.2	44.0	..	10.7
United States	48.9	26.5	8.6	46.4	29.7	8.2
OECD	47.3	27.9	14.5	45.0	27.7	14.0

Note: Nearest year available when a ratio for the year indicated is not available. The shares do not add up to 100 because of other collective services.
1.   Hospital care also includes care in nursing homes.
2.   Some countries include hospitals outpatient services.
Source: OECD (1993), *OECD Health Systems: Facts and Trends, 1960-1991.*

for pharmaceutical drugs (see below). In contrast, a positive feature of the Canadian health system is the relatively low level of public expenditure on administration, both as a share of total expenditure and in per capita terms.

A crucial factor in cost containment is control over the financing of the system, as this means that providers are faced with a monopoly purchaser and in principle allows global budgeting. In some OECD countries where the system is financed by tax revenues, as is the case in Canada, user fees are charged in order to limit demand pressures which may result from such a system. There is no clear correlation between such fees and expenditure levels or utilisation rates, however. This may be because user fees are often very low. Methods of reimbursing providers vary widely. The method of prospective global budgeting, used for financing hospitals in Canada, tends to lead to lower expenditure, although this often stems from greater rationing rather than increased cost-effectiveness (see below). The "fee for service" payment method used in Canada for remunerating physicians (including those practising in hospitals) is generally associated with higher spending.

Together with the Nordic countries (which also have a tax-based system) and Japan (which has a mandatory social-insurance system), Canada has achieved one of the highest standards of equity of access to health services among OECD countries. Governments in most countries, with the notable exception of the United States and Turkey, now offer social coverage to more than 90 per cent of the population for hospital and ambulatory care. In Canada, coverage is universal, with enrolment automatic and free for all residents. As regards pharmaceutical consumption outside of the hospital setting, coverage by public programmes is relatively limited, although co-payments for the services covered are at the low end.

There are, however, other dimensions of access to health care. Lower expenditure levels of public systems can mean that they are more efficient, or that they are more parsimonious than private ones, which would be reflected in waiting lists and admission rates. Reported hospital admission rates show Canada typically in a middle position between two extremes, the United Kingdom and United States.[15] The number of hospital beds per inhabitant is below the OECD average but higher than in both the United Kingdom and the United States. The occupancy rate is relatively high and the average length of stay in hospitals generally low by international comparison. A notable feature is the very low availability of publicly-funded home care services by OECD standards. Nursing home care has remained broadly stable in relation to total expenditure on in-patient care, although the share of persons over 65 in the total population has increased markedly over the past decade.

The performance and cost of the system

Health outcomes

The Canadian health system is often cited as an example, since it combines universal health coverage with cost containment, while achieving good health outcomes. Judging from indicators such as morbidity and infant mortality, it appears that Canada rates above average, although this relative advantage has declined over recent years (Table 2.2). However, the health status of a population is also linked to social, economic and environmental conditions, not just the care system. In this regard, relations between health spending and outcomes appear to be strongest for life expectancy, suggesting that health expenditure may be having most effects in postponing death for the old. Life expectancy – both at birth and for those in the older age groups – has indeed increased dramatically over the past 30 years, with levels in Canada continuing to exceed the OECD average (Table 2.2). Over the past decade, progress in this field has been more limited in Canada, however, than in the OECD area generally. The same is true for prenatal and infant mortality, which – starting from below-average rates – has been greatly reduced, though at diminishing rates. This leads to a suspicion that for countries with a relatively favourable health status of the population, such as Canada, spending additional funds on health care provides fewer tangible benefits. Instead, further improvements in health outcomes may depend to a considerable degree on factors outside the health system, including socio-economic characteristics and the environment.

Table 2.2. **Comparative health outcomes**

		1960	1980	1985	1990
A. Life expectancy					
Canada					
Life expectancy at birth	– male	68.4	71.9	73.0	73.8
	– female	74.3	78.9	79.8	80.4
Life expectancy at age 60	– male	16.8	18.0	18.4	18.9
	– female	19.9	23.0	23.2	23.7
Simple OECD average					
Life expectancy at birth	– male	67.9	67.8	68.9	73.1
	– female	73.0	74.0	75.1	79.4
Life expectancy at age 60	– male	16.3	16.3	16.8	18.3
	– female	19.1	20.4	21.0	22.7
		1960-64	1980-84	1985-89	1990
B. Perinatal and infant mortality [1]					
Canada					
Perinatal mortality		2.8	1.0	0.8	0.8
Infant mortality		2.6	0.9	0.7	0.7
Simple OECD average					
Perinatal mortality		3.0	1.2	0.9	n.a.
Infant mortality		2.8	1.0	0.0	n.a.

1. Per cent of live and still births and live births alone, respectively.
Source: OECD.

Expenditure growth

Overview in an OECD context

Canada's share of health expenditure in GDP has traditionally exceeded the OECD average. What has focused attention on the need for controlling costs is that this gap has widened considerably over the past decade (Diagram 2.3). In 1980, Canada's health spending as a per cent of GDP was the sixth-highest in the OECD area. By the late 1980s, Canada had become the second-highest spender on this measure, behind the United States. In 1991, health expenditure reached 13 and 10 per cent of GDP in the United States and Canada, respectively (13.9 and 10.1 per cent in 1992); this compares with an OECD average of less than 8 per cent. In terms of per capita health spending Canada ranked third at the beginning of the 1980s. Overtaking Sweden in 1987, Canada has now the highest health care expenditures per capita among countries with national health systems.

Per capita health spending across countries is closely linked to per capita income, which explains to a large extent expenditure levels (Diagram 2.4). In this regard, Canada's spending is higher than predicted, though to a more limited extent than in the United States, with this gap increasing if the US is omitted from the sample.[16] Also, re-estimating the equation for the early 1980s shows that the gap has emerged only over the last decade.

International comparisons of health expenditure are usually based on GDP purchasing power parities. However, cross-country comparisons of prices and volumes can also be made using purchasing-power-parity price indices that are specific to health-care although these are considered less reliable. By such measures, the volume of health care per capita in Canada is only the fourth-highest in the OECD area, behind Japan, France and the United States (Diagram 2.5). The different ranking results from relatively low health-care prices in Japan and France and relatively high prices in the United States and – to a lesser degree – in Canada.

To some extent, price differentials reflect the composition of health expenditure. As noted above, the – expensive – hospital sector is relatively important in Canada. The number of physicians per capita is near the OECD average. But there is a clear cross-country relationship between physician income and per capita health-care expenditures, and compensation per physician is among the highest in Canada (whether measured in terms of purchasing power parities, or as a fraction of labour income per worker). However, as can be seen from Diagram 2.6, relative price levels (health care inflation net of

Diagram 2.3. **Health care expenditures**

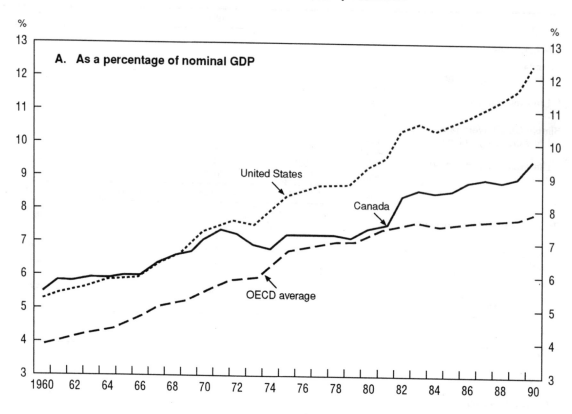

A. As a percentage of nominal GDP

United States

Canada

OECD average

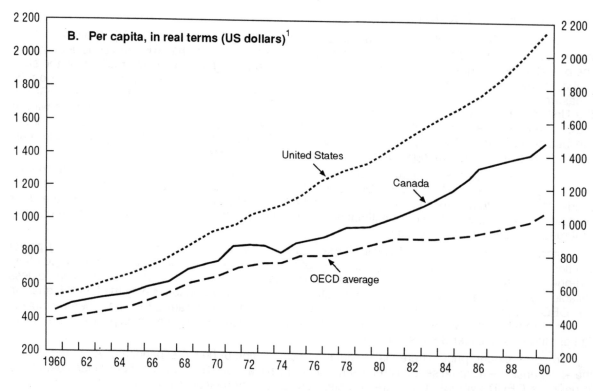

B. Per capita, in real terms (US dollars)[1]

United States

Canada

OECD average

1. Using GDP deflators and purchasing power parities, 1985 dollars.
Source: OECD (1993), *OECD Health System: Facts and Trends, 1960-1991.*

Diagram 2.4. **Health and wealth**

Thousand dollars per capita, 1990 figure[1]

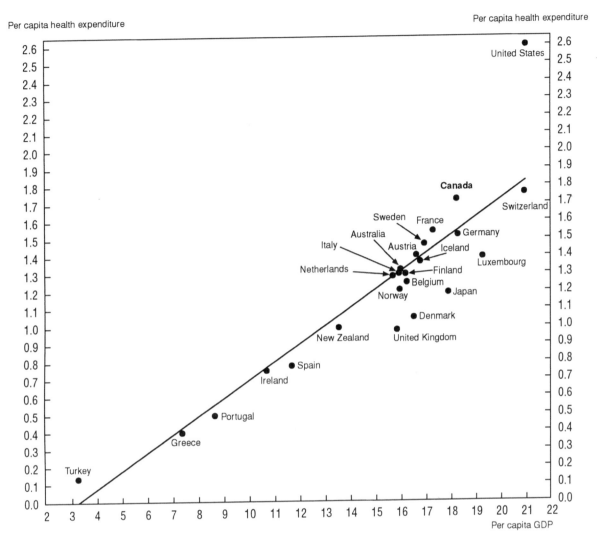

1. Using 1990 purchasing-power-parity exchange rates for GDP.
Source: OECD.

general inflation) reflect to a large extent developments in the 1980s; during this period measured health-specific inflation in the United States and Canada – amounting to about 30 and 20 per cent, respectively – outstripped that of the overall price level. This is in contrast to other countries where health-care prices were generally stable relative to the overall price level. Over this period, relative prices for hospital care and physicians changed little in Canada but the relative price increase for pharmaceutical products exceeded 4 per cent per annum, the highest rate in the OECD area.

While medical-specific inflation in Canada in the 1980s was more than twice as high as the average, real health spending per capita expanded in line with that in the OECD area (Table 2.3). In fact, per capita volume growth has tended to decelerate since the 1960s, although this trend has been less pronounced in Canada than elsewhere. However, with above-average population growth, real health-care expenditure expansion in Canada exceeded the OECD average in the 1980s (Table 2.4). This was not fully offset by slightly higher economic growth, so that the volume share of health spending in GDP expanded more rapidly in Canada than generally elsewhere. Combined with high health-specific

Diagram 2.5. Health care prices and volumes in the OECD area
1990

A. Relative health care prices[1]

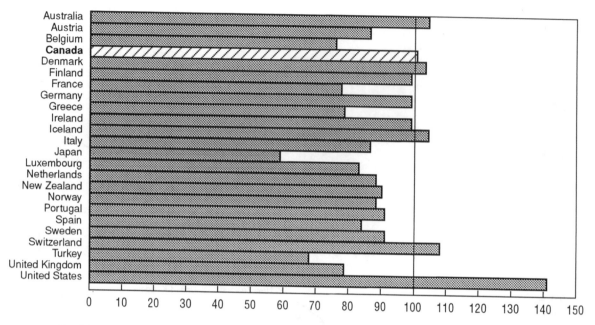

B. Volume of health care per capita[2]

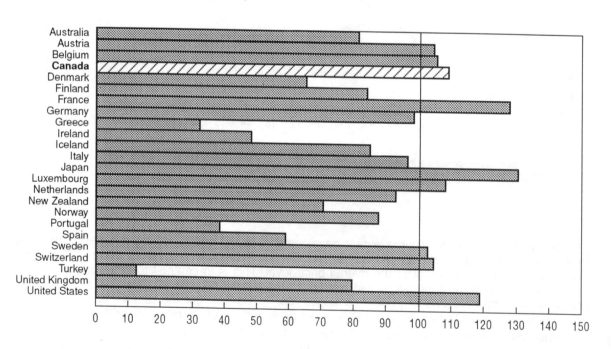

1. Purchasing-power-parity price of household consumption expenditure on health care relative to price of final expenditure on GDP (OECD = 100).
2. Total expenditure on health care in US dollars at purchasing-power-parity exchange rates for household consumption expenditure on health care (OECD = 100).
Source: OECD.

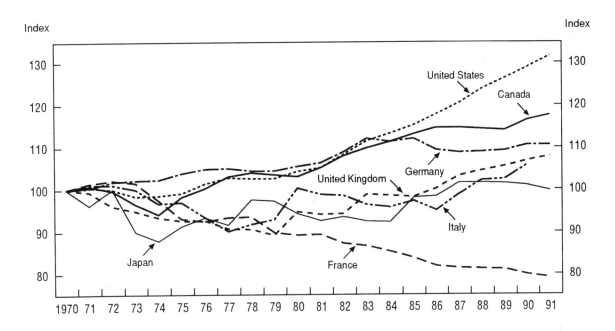

Diagram 2.6. **Trends in the relative price of health care**[1]
International comparison
1970 = 100

1. Deflator for health care expenditure divided by the GDP deflator.
Source: OECD.

inflation this explains the marked increase in the nominal health spending to GDP ratio in Canada by international comparison.

In this context, one factor worth noting is demographic trends. Ageing of the population is likely to cause financing and delivery problems in many OECD countries, as those over the age of 65 consume on average four times more care than the rest of the population. On the basis of the projected increase in the proportion of old people, by early next century these problems should be worst in Japan and Canada.[17]

Table 2.3. **Trends in health inflation and benefits**

Annual rates of increase in per cent

	Medical specific inflation			Real health benefits per capita		
	1960-70	1970-80	1980-90	1960-70	1970-80	1980-90
Canada	1.4	0.3	1.7	4.7	3.8	2.3
France	0.1	−1.5	−0.8	7.6	6.6	4.5
Germany	0.9	1.0	0.6	4.4	5.7	1.1
Italy	1.0	−0.5	0.6	7.8	6.1	3.0
Japan	1.1	−1.1	0.9	12.5	7.7	3.0
United Kingdom	−0.8	−0.6	1.4	4.6	4.9	1.9
United States	0.8	0.1	2.5	5.2	3.8	2.1
OECD	0.9	0.4	0.8	7.0	5.2	2.3

Note: Medical specific inflation is defined as the excess of health care price increases over those on all goods and services. A few 1980-90 rates are projections of a likely outcome, while some 1960-70 and 1970-80 rates may overstate trends because of discontinuities in the underlying time series. They exclude Turkey and, in 1960-70, Luxembourg and Portugal.
Source: OECD.

39

Table 2.4. **Decomposition of health expenditure growth**

Average annual rates of increase in per cent, 1980-90

	Share of total expenditure on health in GDP 1980	Nominal health expenditure growth	Health deflator growth	Total domestic expenditure price deflator	Medical specific price increases	Health care volume growth	Population growth	Per capita health benefit growth	Share of total expenditure on health in GDP 1990
Canada	7.3	10.7	6.9	5.1	1.7	3.4	1.0	2.3	9.4
France	7.5	10.4	5.2	6.0	−0.8	5.0	0.5	4.5	8.8
Germany	8.4	4.6	3.3	2.6	0.6	1.3	0.2	1.1	8.6
Italy	6.6	14.2	10.7	10.0	0.6	3.2	0.2	3.0	7.7
Japan	6.5	6.0	2.4	1.5	0.9	3.6	0.6	3.0	6.7
United Kingdom	5.9	9.8	7.6	6.1	1.4	2.1	0.2	1.9	6.1
United States	9.3	10.3	6.9	4.3	2.5	3.1	1.0	2.1	12.2
OECD	7.0	11.8	8.7	7.9	0.8	2.8	0.5	2.3	7.8

Note: Medical specific inflation is defined as the excess of health care price increases over those on all goods and services. A few 1990 ratios and 1980-90 rates are projections of a likely outcome. The underlying statistical series are consistent for the full decade but unobserved discontinuities cannot be precluded. They exclude Turkey.
Source: OECD (1993), *OECD Health Systems: Facts and Trends, 1960-1991.*

Key determinants

i) Quantity of health care

Since 1960 the rise in health care expenditure adjusted for general price inflation, reflects increases in per capita use of medical services (one-half), medical price increases in excess of general price rises (one-quarter), and population growth (one-quarter). Growth in the volume of health services supplied per capita has outstripped that of real per capita GDP, the former averaging 4.6 per cent per annum, compared to 2.8 per cent for the latter (Diagram 2.7). However, this margin has been uniform neither over time nor across service types. The largest divergence between real health expenditure and GDP growth occurred in the 1960s, before narrowing significantly in subsequent decades.

Although the narrowing of the divergence coincides with the gradual shift toward the national medicare system – completed in the early 1970s – it does not result from firmer expenditure controls across all health services.[18] Real expenditure growth in hospitals remained consistently above that of GDP during the 1960-70 period, prior to the introduction of global budgeting, after which the trend reversed. In contrast, real expenditure growth in both pharmaceuticals and physician costs continued to outstrip that of GDP throughout the entire period. These are areas where government has exercised only limited cost control. The volume of nursing-care and ambulatory services has also risen significantly throughout the 1980s, in response to both underlying demand pressure from a growing elderly population, and more recently, policy decisions to de-institutionalise health care-services (Table 2.5).

ii) Price of health care

A similar pattern, both over time and across health categories, emerges with regard to price changes. Health price inflation outstripped that of the consumer price index (CPI) for the entire period 1960-91, averaging 6.6 per cent per annum in the former compared to 5.2 per cent for the latter (Diagram 2.8, Table 2.6). This is largely driven by hospital prices, of which 60 per cent are wages, and during the 1980s rising pharmaceutical prices. Health sector wage growth consistently outpaced economy-wide settlements throughout the 1970s, before falling more into line during the 1980s – the decade in which health price inflation has most closely followed that of the CPI. However, this has been offset by the rapid growth in the price of pharmaceuticals over the 1980s, which averaged 9.6 per cent per annum after remaining subdued over the two previous decades. Factors deemed to explain the rise in pharmaceutical prices include the high introductory price of drugs, modest increases in existing drug prices and shifting drugs within therapeutic classes to higher priced categories.[19]

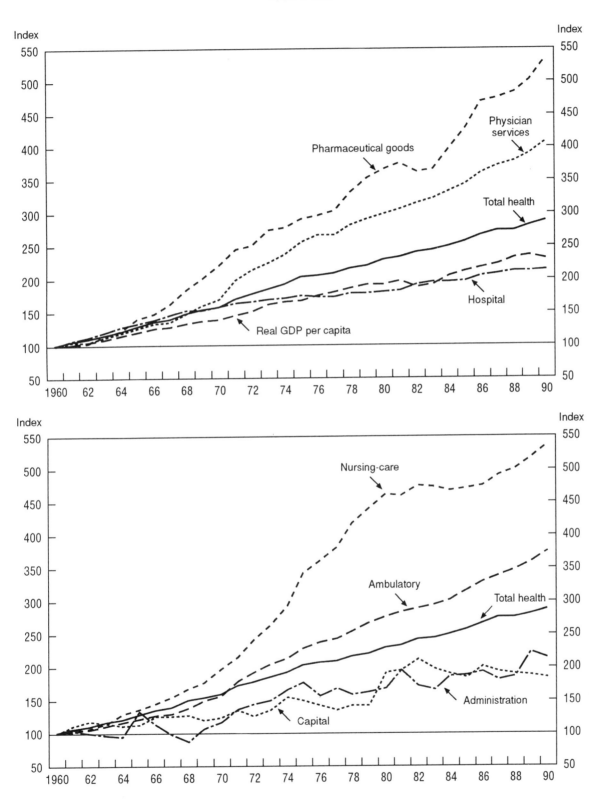

Diagram 2.7. **Real per capita health expenditure by component**
1960 = 100

Source: OECD.

41

Table 2.5. **Real per capita health expenditure by component**

Average annual percentage change

	1960-70	1970-80	1980-90
Total health expenditure	4.7	3.8	3.5
Real GDP per capita	3.3	3.3	1.9
Hospitals	4.7	1.4	1.7
Physician services	5.5	5.8	3.2
Ambulatory care	4.5	5.9	3.1
Nursing care	7.0	8.9	1.5
Capital	2.1	4.5	-0.3
Administration	1.5	3.7	2.5

Source: OECD.

Table 2.6. **Health price inflation by component**

Average annual percentage change

	1960-70	1970-80	1980-90
Total health	4.5	8.3	6.9
CPI	2.7	8.0	5.9
Hospitals	6.4	10.9	6.8
Ambulatory	4.0	6.0	6.2
Physician services	3.7	5.3	6.1
Pharmaceuticals	-0.4	4.5	9.6

Source: OECD.

Diagram 2.8. **The relative price of health by component**[1]

1960 = 100

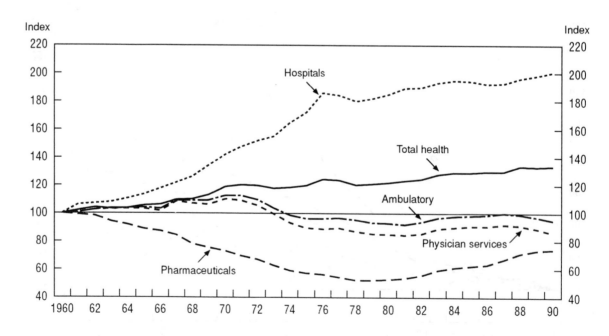

1. Deflated using the consumer price index.
Source: OECD.

42

iii) Aggregate expenditure

In discussing aggregate health expenditure, it is important to separate the level of spending from its trend-growth, facilitating the identification of both current and future cost pressure. As physician payments and hospital outlays constitute the largest components of health expenditure (Diagram 2.9), recent attention with regard to their containment is not surprising. Expenditure growth in both components has increased at an annual average rate of approximately 11.5 per cent since 1960, well in excess of the 9.8 per cent averaged for nominal GDP. However, expenditure on the former – as a ratio of total health expenditure – has remained relatively stable since the 1970s, at around 15 per cent, while the latter has declined from its peak of approximately 45 per cent in 1970 to its current level of 40 per cent.

A large proportion of the relative expenditure decline for hospitals is explained by the substitution toward non-institutional community based care, for example, nursing homes and ambulatory services. Expenditure growth on non-institutional health services has averaged 14 per cent per annum since 1960 – in part reflecting its low starting base – and now accounts for over 10 per cent of total health expenditure. Likewise, pharmaceutical expenditure grew faster than aggregate health expenditure, averaging 12 per cent per annum since 1960. Expenditure on pharmaceuticals is the only component to have accelerated during the 1980s, to an average of over 15 per cent per annum, and now accounts for roughly 13.5 per cent of total health expenditure.

As noted earlier, a positive feature of the Canadian health system is its relatively low administrative costs with respect to both its level and growth trend. Administrative expenditure[20] has declined as a proportion of total health expenditure for the last 30 years, from 2.7 per cent in 1960 to only 1.2 per cent in 1990, indicating significant economies of scale. Likewise, the share of expenditure on capital equipment has also decreased throughout this period, both as a percentage of total health expenditure – from 10 per cent in 1960 to 4 per cent in 1990 – and in relation to nominal GDP. This highlights both the initial high level of infrastructure development in the 1960s – especially hospitals – and the more stringent budgeting methods established for capital expenditure.

In summary, both price and quantity growth underlie the rising share of health expenditure relative to GDP. The growth of expenditure components – excluding administration and capital equipment – has outstripped that of GDP on average since 1960, with this margin widening in the 1980s. In terms of contribution, hospital expenditure remains the largest, with labour costs being the driving force (Diagram 2.9). Controls on physician costs have been relatively unsuccessful – primarily due to the absence of volume controls on the number of services offered as well as growth in the number of physicians – while expenditure on pharmaceuticals remains a relatively unregulated component of growing cost pressure.

Problems with the Canadian health system

This section outlines some of the main problems facing the Canadian health system. Although for the sake of analysis they have been separated into demand and supply factors, the distinction is sometimes unclear, especially with regard to supply-induced demand. The demand aspects are common across all OECD countries to varying degrees, whereas supply-side considerations are more determined by the specific organisational structure. In the case of Canada, it appears that the latter are responsible for the majority of rising cost pressures.

Demand aspects

Several key demand-side features help explain the rise in health expenditure. They include a high income elasticity of demand, moral hazard issues for both patients and physicians, and an ageing population. First, the income elasticity of nominal health expenditure is estimated to have averaged around 1.2 over the 1960-91 period, having remained relatively constant between the two time periods 1960-75 and 1975-91 (representing periods pre- and post-universal health care). However, this result is due more to the rise in the price, rather than volume, of health services – with increasingly expensive health care being demanded. This is illustrated by the fall in the elasticity of real (inflation adjusted) health expenditure with respect to GDP (on a per capita basis), from 1.3 between 1960-75 to 1.1 during 1976-91.

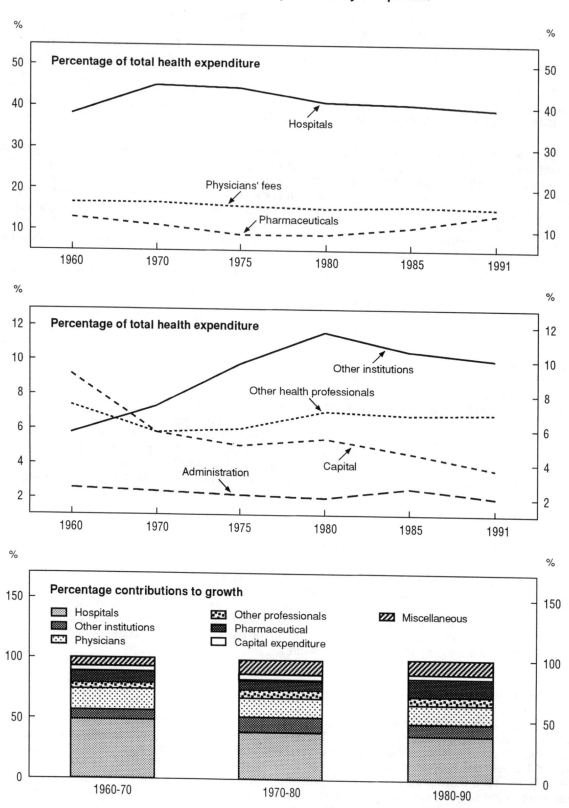

Diagram 2.9. **Health expenditure by component**

Percentage of total health expenditure

Hospitals

Physicians' fees

Pharmaceuticals

Percentage of total health expenditure

Other institutions

Other health professionals

Capital

Administration

Percentage contributions to growth

Hospitals
Other institutions
Physicians
Other professionals
Pharmaceutical
Capital expenditure
Miscellaneous

1960-70   1970-80   1980-90

Source: OECD.

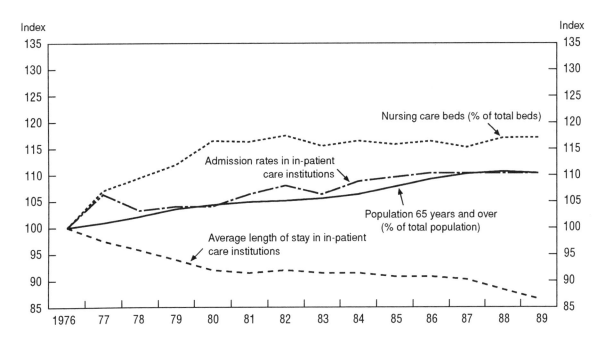

Diagram 2.10. **Elderly health care commitments**
1976 = 100

Source: OECD.

The issue of moral hazard, although not unique to Canada, poses one of the more persistent obstacles to containing health care costs. A universal insurance system implies zero marginal costs to both the provider (physician) and consumer (patient) of health services. This means the marginal benefit of treatment can remain below its marginal cost at the quantity of health services consumed, implying an over-consumption or misallocation of health resources. However, if the price elasticity of demand for health services is low and combined with some quantity rationing, the extent of over-consumption will remain limited. Nevertheless, price elasticities are estimated to vary across health service type, with for example, a larger elasticity found for community health care services than for hospitals.[21] This implies a growing risk of over-consumption as health delivery trends continue to move toward the former.

Increased costs – especially those of hospitals – are also positively associated with Canada's ageing population. However, it is unclear how significant this has been in aggregate terms. For example, although longer stays and more frequent visits by the elderly have increased expenditure, this has been largely offset by lower costs within other age groups, including a lower birth rate and shorter hospital stays (Diagram 2.10). At present the most pressing concern with regard to the ageing population is the increasing intensity and associated costs of health services demanded (see below).

Supply considerations

The main supply-side factors explaining the increase in health expenditure in Canada include moral hazard and supply-induced demand, the declining productivity trend, and the cost of inputs (such as technology, labour and pharmaceuticals). Importantly, these features are all linked to the organisational structure of the Canadian health system. The problem of supply-induced demand stems from the asymmetrical nature of information within the system, enabling physicians to determine both the supply and demand of health services provided. This is augmented by the fee-for-service payment system, which encourages increased service intensity by removing physicians' cost accountability. For example, although physician numbers grew by 20 per cent during the 1980s, only modest pressure arose on their income growth, highlighting physicians' ability to offset competitive pressures on fee-levels by increasing the throughput of services (Diagram 2.11). Other concerns regarding the fee-for-service method include the high transaction costs of negotiation, the conflict created between management and physicians when operating within global budgets, and the bias toward increased technology usage (see below). It becomes apparent that while payments to physicians are an important direct cost, just as important is how physicians interact with other resources in the health sector. Their method of practice significantly affects not only the employment of other resources but also the input costs into the sector.

Despite the significant difficulties involved in measuring the "output" of hospitals – especially gauging its quality[22] – declining hospital productivity appears a source of rising cost pressure.[23] Rising labour resources, promoted by an increase in service intensity, is a significant contributor to this trend (Diagram 2.12). Auer (1987) estimates that approximately 30 per cent of the rise in hospital expenditure between 1960 and 1980 can be explained by increased service intensity alone. This is split roughly one-third to increased case-intensity – the number of services performed per patient – and two-thirds to increased task intensity – inputs per service performed. Indeed, even if quality concerns were accounted for in the measurement of health outcomes (potentially leading to a significant rise), issues concerning the relative productivity of alternative treatments remain. This is especially relevant with regard to long-term care in different institutional environments.

The number of staff-per-bed has risen constantly since the 1960s, with this likely to continue over the medium-term given the lagged influence regulation has over labour inputs. Current physician requirements were initially estimated in the 1960s on the basis of inflated population growth projections. This led to a continuous increase in the number of physicians per population, with the ratio of inhabitants per physician falling from around 860 to 450 between 1960 and 1990. This has been matched by growth in the nursing staff, with the ratio of inhabitants to registered nurses falling from 170 in 1971 to 120 by 1991 (Diagram 2.12).

Personnel costs constitute the largest single component (75 per cent) of total health expenditure. In addition to the expansion in aggregate physician payments, the growth in nurses' wages has outpaced the economy-wide average since 1960. This is partially explained by their relative short supply in the 1960-70s, and more recently by the rise in their average skill levels. Physicians' average net income in 1992 also remains the highest of four comparable professional groups, including dentists (1.16 times higher), lawyers (1.25 times higher), and accountants (1.6 times higher). More recently, however, the growth rate of physicians' income relative to these groups has declined (Diagram 2.12).

Recent progress in health technology appears to have intensified cost pressures. The growth in health technology has increasingly implied more labour hours-per-patient, with most technology-substitution being limited to adopting different treatments for the same medical problem (Diagram 2.13). Although some substitution has occurred between methods of health delivery – for example, increased home rather than hospital based care – even this is ambiguous with regard to cost-saving, with the freed hospital bed often subsequently filled by patients previously outside of institutional care and in need of more intensive care. More general problems include the pace of technological change being too rapid to benefit from economies of scale and the discovery of new treatments for previously intractable problems implying new costs. These cost-raising factors are consolidated by physicians' fee-for-service payment system. This promotes the use of increasingly high-technology medicine – given that doctors are not liable for the costs, but can claim the financial benefits – removing any incentive to consider the marginal cost-benefit trade-off of specific treatments. The latter practice is further constrained by the lack of appropriate data (see below).

Summary

On balance, factors outside of the organisation structure of the health system – including demographic and income trends – appear unable to explain the bulk of the rise in health care costs. Instead, supply-side explanations dominate, themselves endemic to the structure of the health industry. These include rising input costs (especially labour and pharmaceuticals) and declining productivity as resource intensity grows (especially technology usage). Funding and budgeting techniques, and both physician numbers and their mode of payment, appear central determinants in lowering efficiency incentives, promoting supply-induced demand, and increasing service intensity. Furthermore, the reliance on quantitative budget controls alone is limited in its the ability to encourage efficiency gains. Hospital budget caps fail to address underlying cost pressures, are inflexible in responding to changing demand patterns,[24] and remain geared toward rewarding those who spend most.

Diagram 2.11. **Physician costs**

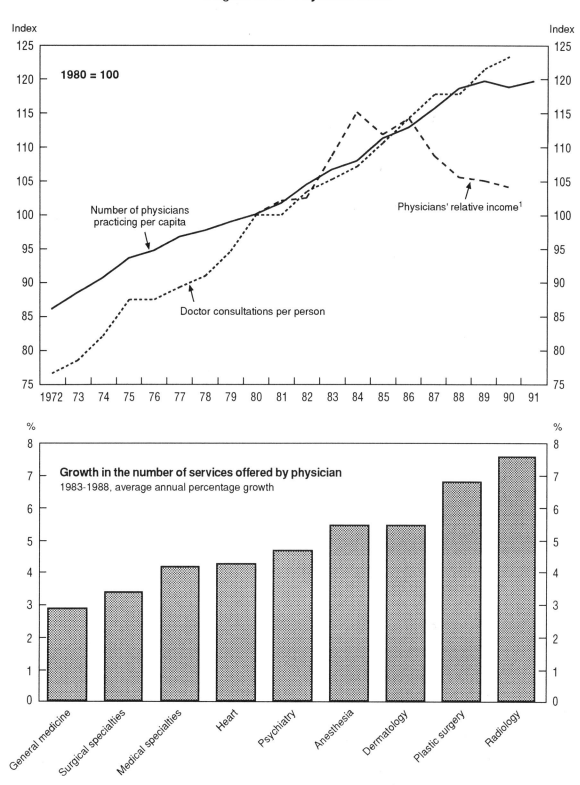

Index

125

120

1980 = 100

115

110

105

100

Number of physicians
practicing per capita

Physicians' relative income[1]

95

90

85

Doctor consultations per person

80

75

1972 73 74 75 76 77 78 79 80 81 82 83 84 85 86 87 88 89 90 91

%

8

7 **Growth in the number of services offered by physician**
1983-1988, average annual percentage growth

6

5

4

3

2

1

0

General medicine | Surgical specialties | Medical specialties | Heart | Psychiatry | Anesthesia | Dermatology | Plastic surgery | Radiology

1. Ratio: average net physician income/average net income of dentists, lawyers and accountants.
Sources: Ministry of Finance; OECD.

Diagram 2.12. **Labour costs in the health sector**

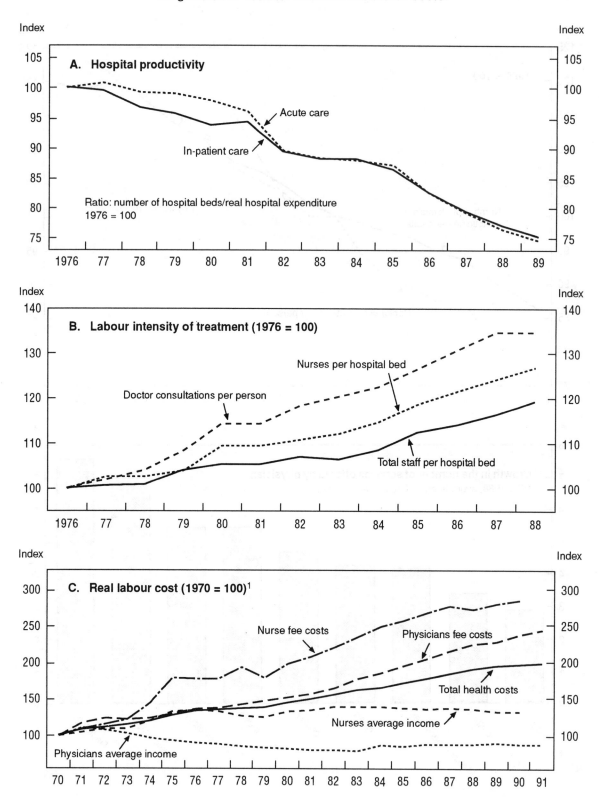

1. Deflated by the private consumption index.
Source: OECD.

Diagram 2.13. **Technology intensity of health services**
Real expenditure per in-patient care bed
1971 = 100

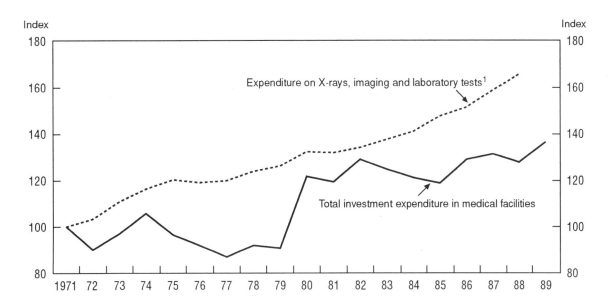

1. Deflated by the medical and health expenditure price index.
Source: OECD.

On the demand-side, the lack of clear price signals lowers consumers' accountability and may potentially induce over-consumption. The aggregate outcome is increased health costs-per-patient, driven by an ongoing rise in the intensity of health care services. It seems that the problems of the current system are not related to its "publicness" *per se*, but rather the incentive structures that are inherent in the system (see Diagram 2.14).

In sum, the system – in aiming for a balance between equity, autonomy and expenditure control – has struggled to adjust to changing population needs and to manage resource distribution effectively. Administrators are left with three possible solutions: accommodate the rising health costs with increased resources; implement further blanket cost controls; or reorganise the delivery system to promote increased efficiency. Of these options a mixture of the latter two appears most reasonable and largely characterises recent attempts to contain costs.

Improving the system: reforms to date and future strategies

Recent policy actions

Overview

During the 1980s rising health expenditure induced a progressive shift of impetus away from issues of access and affordability, toward cost control. With the limits in federal transfers to provinces being approached in the late 1980s,[25] a consensus amongst provinces emerged that health care expenditure was absorbing a sufficient proportion of aggregate GDP, and that initiatives were required to manage the health system more effectively – especially in order to preserve the principles of the Canada Health Act. This has led to a focus both on cost control and efficiency gains, especially with regard to the needs of the elderly, technology change, the number, mix, and reimbursement of human resources, as well as an increased emphasis on research and evaluation of treatment, and on improving the dissemination of

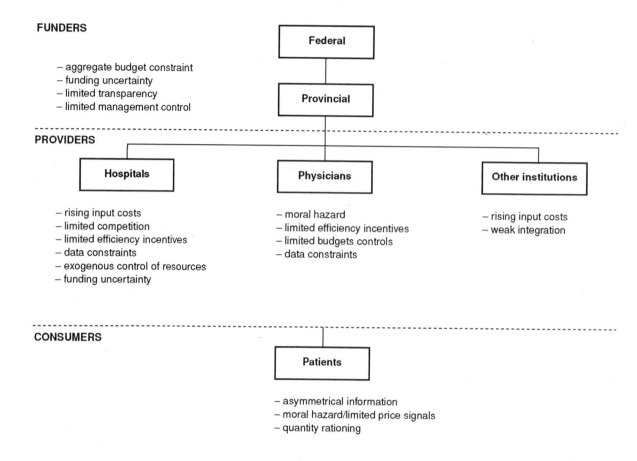

Diagram 2.14. **A summary of problems**

FUNDERS

Federal

Provincial

– aggregate budget constraint
– funding uncertainty
– limited transparency
– limited management control

PROVIDERS

Hospitals

Physicians

Other institutions

– rising input costs
– limited competition
– limited efficiency incentives
– data constraints
– exogenous control of resources
– funding uncertainty

– moral hazard
– limited efficiency incentives
– limited budgets controls
– data constraints

– rising input costs
– weak integration

CONSUMERS

Patients

– asymmetrical information
– moral hazard/limited price signals
– quantity rationing

The current health systems shortcomings are highlighted in this diagram, allocated according to funders – the federal and provincial governments; providers – hospitals, physicians, and other medical services; and consumers – the public or patients.

– *Funders:* the problem here is one of controlling expenditure, which has led to expenditure off-loading onto provincial governments and associated provincial budget uncertainty. The use of general tax revenue also reduces consumer and provider price awaneress and accountability. The funding technique also results in a lack of detailed cost information on which future marginal-benefit analysis could be hinged.
– *Providers:* hospitals remain limited in their incentives to promote efficiency gains in excess of their budget cap. This results from the weak interface with other non-hospital providers, limited control over the intensity of resource use – which is instead determined by physicians, the absence of detailed cost information and the current funding techniques. For physicians, efficiency concerns are largely removed through their payment methodology, which also biases toward increased service intensity and fails to control income growth. Community-based health services remain limited given the absence of binding links between their cost-effectiveness and patient loading.
– *Consumer:* the major problem is related to moral hazard in the absence of price signals. The physician determines both the type and level of treatment, while the consumer is largely unaware of both its appropriateness or cost.

this information. Three general themes have developed: *a)* an increase in consultation between interest groups with regard to the future of health provision, *b)* a shift away from the ongoing expansion of health services towards consolidation and innovation in funding, and *c)* a shift in delivery toward community oriented prevention and health promotion.

a)   Enhancing stakeholder consultation

During recent years more emphasis has been placed on a wider concept of "health" including promotion and disease prevention. This is reflected in the organisation structure of government departments, with the creation of promotion and prevention units, and in some provinces the creation of strategic planning units to co-ordinate health policy. Provincial governments'increased willingness to consult publicly is best demonstrated by the almost unanimous – across provinces – publication of health system reviews during the 1980s. The policy recommendations all included a greater focus on health promotion and disease prevention, community-based care alternatives, and increased accountability. Recent examples of consultation between governments and stakeholders include Ontario establishing a "Framework Agreement" – committing the government and physicians to work co-operatively – and Alberta establishing an "Urban Hospital Council" – formalising the government-stakeholder consultation processes. "Health Advisory Councils" have also been established in several provinces, facilitating medium to long-term planning advice to the Minister of Health from a broad spectrum of society. In addition, local health planning entities such as "District Health Councils" are being revitalised, although control over allocating the health budget generally remains with the provincial government.[26] However, Quebec is pursuing a more aggressive approach with the devolution of budget control – excluding physician salaries – to similar regional boards (see Annex).

b) Service consolidation and funding innovation

As mentioned earlier, federal contributions to the health system were restrained in 1991 by the capping of transfers to the provinces until 1995. Similarly, although only limited change has occurred in hospital funding techniques – following the move from line-by-line to global budgeting – there has been general tightening in budgets on a "no deficits" policy basis throughout the late 1980s. Furthermore, some provinces have begun experimenting with their budget practices to enhance efficiency incentives, for example, allowing surpluses to be carried over into the following year, or adjusting acute care funding to reflect local population needs or severity of illness.[27]

Regular performance reviews and institutional comparisons are also intensifying – both mandatory and voluntary. Mandatory reviews include the Minister of Finance's annual audits, statistical surveys by Statistics Canada, and performance reviews by the Hospital Medical Records Institute (HMRI). The latter two provide data on resource use and comparative costs. Voluntary reviews include the Canadian Council on Health Facilities Accreditation (CCHFA), who monitor quality control, and the Management Information Services (MIS) group, who provide data comparisons between institutions and suggest improved management techniques. The National Physicians Data Base (NPDB) also surveys physicians' practices for comparative purposes.

The provincial monopoly-funding position has also facilitated the rationalisation of services to avoid duplication, especially in larger urban areas. Regional planning boards (see above) have generally been given the responsibility for determining service requirements. Furthermore, a registry of available acute care beds is also being developed to assist in the placement of patients and reduce waiting time. With regard to labour costs, many provinces have recently introduced stringent wage controls affecting all public service workers – in which nurses are included. Finally there are moves to co-ordinate better the various organisations (see above) involved in data collection.[28] This could eventually lead to the development of unique patient identifiers standardised across provinces, containing financial, utilisation, demographic and health status statistics.

Progress has likewise been made with regard to capping physician payments, although this varies across provinces. Five provinces[29] have now negotiated a cap on physician remuneration, although maintaining the fee-for-service payment method. These caps generally reduce payments for services provided beyond an expenditure limit, in an attempt to control service-intensity. Alternative funding methods being explored include: salaried positions, payments per session, contracting care in emergency and long-term care institutions, and capitation payments. Committees such as the Advisory Committee on Health Human Resources (ACHHR) and the Advisory Committee on Institutional and Medical Services (ACIMS) (now superseded by the Health Services Committee) represent efforts to improve the efficiency of health distribution. The National Health Research and Development Program (NHRDP) is likewise charged with analysing innovative funding and delivery mechanisms, as well as measuring "health outputs". With regard to physician numbers, a provincial agreement was reached in early 1992 on the necessity and means of limiting their growth. This takes the form of restricting medical school entry and reducing post-graduate medical enrolments.

With regard to rising pharmaceutical costs, the Patented Medicines Review Board (PMRB) was established in 1987 with a mandate to protect consumers from excess drug price increases, summarise pricing trends, and report on research and development activity. The Ministry of Health is also attempting to improve drug management through the proposed Canadian Agency for Pharmaceuticals Information Assessment (CAPIA). The focus here is on the cost-effectiveness of medicines, largely as a guide for formulary decisions.[30] At the same time, a number of provincial governments are amending their supplementary health benefits, primarily by reducing the range of pharmaceutical coverage, increasingly restricting access to benefits according to individuals' means, and introducing small co-payment fees.[31] Technology assessment has also received attention in the late 1980s, with the establishment of the Canadian Co-ordinating Office on Health Technology (CCOHTA). Its goal is to encourage the appropriate use of technology via the collection, analysis and dissemination of information concerning the effectiveness and cost of competing technologies.

c) Improved community services

Some of the major efficiency reforms of recent years have occurred in the delivery of community-based care and health promotion. The 1986 federal government report "Achieving Health for All" led to collaboration between interrelated social services across provinces, with national strategies being developed in the areas of drug abuse, tobacco, HIV/AIDS prevention, heart disease, health promotion and the environment. Partnerships were also established between provincial governments, non-government organisations, health providers and research institutes to implement these projects. The NHRDP, created in the early 1970s research health delivery mechanisms, has since been supported by several provincially funded pilot schemes.

Many examples of non-institutional health delivery now exist. These include early discharge programmes and the increased provision of health services at home. Three provinces currently operate such systems in an effort to improve the quality of care by promoting patient independence. These have so far led to lower overhead costs per-patient, although as stated earlier this may not always be the case.[32] Minimising institutional long-term care of the elderly is also a general goal. Independent health facilities (often multiservice) have become more common, where privately owned clinics provide surgical and medical services. Technology growth is a key factor facilitating their expansion, with Ontario recently providing legislation for their control and limited funding. "Single point of entry" systems – which aim to ensure that patients are treated at the most efficient and appropriate level – are also developing. Their key feature is an integrated access system through referral and assessment processes.

Adequacy

When assessing the health-system in general, some useful points of reference include the adequacy and accessibility of necessary care, income protection, and the efficiency of delivery. The Canadian system scores highly in the first two areas, largely as a result of adhering to the Canada Health Act. However, in the desire to adhere to the principles of the Act, some compromises may have occurred with regard to efficiency. Most recent reforms have necessitated the government taking a wider view of health care and increasingly promoting community-based care, funding innovation, partnerships with stakeholders, new government structures, and the devolution of budgets.

Despite some recent success in containing expenditure growth and enhancing efficiency incentives,[33] the reforms to date have generally fallen short of tackling some of the major underlying causes of cost-pressure, namely, the unwillingness to fully utilise the expenditure control a single-payer system allows and the lack of accountability amongst important stakeholders. For example, although federal transfer caps are in place, the federal and provincial funding methods remain largely unchanged, implying an ongoing lack of accountability and transparency amongst providers and consumers. Likewise, it is only more recently that global budgets have become enforced effectively.

Furthermore, despite progress being made with regard to controlling the future growth of physician numbers and progress in implementing physician income caps, it remains unclear how these changes will enhance physicians' accountability with regard to appropriate treatment and delivery-type. The numerous cost comparisons between treatment-types, hospitals, physicians, and other delivery modes, also often fail to be binding (when they are available), reducing internal competition between health providers. Consumers also continue to lack relative price signals for many aspects of health consumption, leaving open the issue of moral hazard. Meanwhile, the ongoing devolution of health resource management – although positive in terms of accountability and flexibility – introduces a risk of increased administration costs and bureaucracy, as well as rent-seeking activity by vested interest groups at the regional level, further stifling allocative efficiency. Finally, despite considerable progress being made in collecting health-related data, the current plethora of institutions gathering, assessing, and disseminating information (see above) appear in need of co-ordination, with steps in this direction now being made. Indeed, the current lack of data arises partly from the narrow concept of "health" historically taken – which excludes information concerning population and socio-economic characteristics – and the lack of systematic patient monitoring – itself a characteristic of the present funding method.

Scope for further progress

Following from the increased consultation between the stakeholders and governments over the late 1980s, there appears to exist a general consensus that efficiency enhancement should be the focus for future reform. However, an important caveat to this is that the reforms take place within the principles of the Canada Health Act – implying the continuance of the national health insurance principles as a precondition for further change. This leaves only a limited role for market forces[34] although some scope for policies such as "managed competition" (see below). Hence, the focus of reform is likely to remain on how the current system can best allocate resources, albeit with changes to the incentive structures. Nevertheless, aggregate cost-containment may continue to depend on the monopoly funding position of the government, meaning that the co-operation of stakeholders remains necessary to ensure that other goals are achieved – such as quality, cost effectiveness, and professional satisfaction from participants in the health sector. At present, most suggested reforms have focused on implementing user-charges, reducing the services deemed "necessary", and maintaining or contracting the level of health budgets. This is especially so as competing pressures on provincial revenues increase.

Strengthening cost containment

The governments' position as single-payer in the health system proves its most valuable policy instrument for containing costs. However, the exploitation of this situation has often failed to reach its full potential. This stems from two key factors: the failure to enforce a binding constraint, and the use of aggregate budget controls alone to motivate efficiency gains. A lesson from the previous two decades is that for a cost containment policy to be binding, it must be comprehensive, because partial regulation is easily evaded or offset. Unlike in the case of hospitals, physicians have remained free of global budget caps. Hence, the introduction of limits on fees simply led to an increase in the volume of services supplied. Furthermore, even the Quebec authorities – who introduced further controls at both the collective and individual physician levels (see Annex) – have not tackled the growth in the number of physicians until recently. Given that the recent reduction in medical-school enrolments will be effective only in the medium term, some form of global cap on physician incomes may yet prove necessary.

Likewise, when establishing a cost-containment framework, the rules must be stringent. The enforcement of hospital budgets has varied considerably over the last decade, both across provinces and over time, ranging from virtual non-enforcement to, more recently, full compliance. It appears that the reluctance to implement cost controls strictly results from the fear that the quality and availability of care will be compromised. In this case, a vital component to global cost containment is to nurture a partnership between all stakeholders. In doing so there is a clear need to improve the incentives for compliance to fixed budgets, especially by rewarding efficiency. A positive example is the authorisation to hospital administrators to carry forward part of any budget surplus into the following fiscal year. Nevertheless, such cost containment policies still fail to discriminate according to local needs. One step toward resolving this would be to allocate budgets according to future expected needs, as opposed to current consumption behaviour. To this end, one could identify regional population characteristics – such as age, sex, location, and environment indicators – and then allocate population-adjusted budgets regionally, providing both efficiency and equity gains.[35] This could be undertaken by the revitalised "District Health Councils" in many provinces. Indeed, most provinces have adopted or are now adopting regional approaches to governance, budgeting and/or priority setting.

Enhancing efficiency

Concerning efficiency, it is important not to separate the role of cost-containment from that of organisational reform, with the two being mutually dependent. The introduction of market-type mechanisms is an often discussed method of ensuring efficiency gains. However, in the absence of accurate output and price measures in the health sector, greatest focus remains on the logic of producers' activities, and to what extent these actions enhance efficiency. Since the health sector remains amenable neither to complete regulation, nor to full corporate sector management techniques, a hybrid of market-type mechanisms has developed. These range from accounting techniques borrowed from the corporate sector[36] to the introduction of managed competition between institutions.

Champagne and his colleagues (1993) identify three forms of organisation that encompass all health systems (technocratic, professional self-regulation, and *laissez-faire*), between which several hybrids exist, including public competition (see below). To date, most reforms have fallen into either the technocratic (increased regulation) or *laissez-faire* (de-insurance of services) categories, with limited focus on structural reorganisation. This raises the concern that only temporary respite from cost pressures have been provided, in the absence of a change to the underlying incentive structures. Such reforms provide few positive incentives to managers and potentially reduce flexibility, while raising administration costs. Another concern is that, by continuing in such a manner, physician autonomy will decline – as defined by their freedom to decide treatment type. Future proposed changes should instead reconcile attempts to rationalise on resources while maintaining physician autonomy, promoting stakeholder participation, and preserving current institution dynamics. Some features of managed care models, especially public competition, provide promising aspects of reform – without compromising the principles of the 1984 Health Act.

Four general areas exist for the introduction of market-type mechanisms, although all are inter-linked. These are: the scope and type of *individual* health insurance provided, *physicians'* operating environment, the *institutional* framework, and the relationship between the *patient and provider*. At the *individual* level, Canada remains at one extreme of the health-insurance spectrum, with the government acting as the single insurer and providing complete coverage for necessary health care. However, there may be some scope for either increased charges – or at least the levying of more transparent "health premiums" – as a means of minimising over-consumption. The underlying rationale is that *a)* user charges raise individuals' accountability to take precaution against ill-health, and *b)* they create an incentive to reduce unnecessary consumption, the magnitude being dependent on the relevant price elasticities.

However, the net benefits of user charges may not be as unambiguous as described above. For example, they are most effective only when the consumer is capable of making an informed choice among therapeutically equivalent service packages, which is often not the case. They can also lead to a reduction in the consumption of necessary health care, increasing costs at a later date. Furthermore, if the price-elasticity is low, then the introduction of user charges may have only a one-off effect on the level of health expenditure, leaving the rate of growth unchanged. A distinction should also be made between differential and uniform user charges. A uniform user fee is more likely to affect the level, rather than the direction of spending, implying fewer efficiency gains. Likewise, differential fees have merit only if they lead to desired steering effects (substitution towards the most efficient provider and/or the most efficient treatment); if they instead deter access to medically necessary services, their advantages could be outweighed by their disadvantages. For user charges to be most effective, offsetting practices by providers and patients must also be minimised. These include inducements, other than price, to ensure consumption levels are maintained, as well as consumers switching to medicines that are provided free of charge.[37] Finally, it is important to focus on total health expenditure, not just the public component, when assessing competitiveness aspects. Should increased user charges result in growing private health coverage – either by employers or employees – this represents a potential labour cost.[38]

As a result, the introduction of differential user charges alone will be insufficient to guarantee efficiency in the health sector. However, this is not to deny that an increased role may exist for them, albeit for services with specific characteristics. Nevertheless, differential user charges should form only a part of a general effort to raise consumer awareness, with for example, the introduction of health premiums being viewed as a complementary – albeit less direct – link between consumption and cost.

The nature of *physicians'* operating environment remains an important area for cost containment in the case of Canada. The criteria for physician resource policy should focus on the "effectiveness" of treatment. The areas of consideration here include physicians' number and skill mix, information provision and use, reimbursement, licensing and regulation, as well as spatial location. The capacity and mix of physicians is concerned with resource requirements. A positive start has been made in this regard with provincial co-operation on reducing medical student numbers. However, to ensure a more equitable distribution of physicians further measures may be required. These could include pre-commit-ting students to geographic regions, providing non-financial inducements – such as amenity policies for dependents, improving support networks, and shifting to regional capitation payments with positive financial inducements (see Annex). With regard to medical information, an increased effort may be necessary to provide the public with accessible information regarding treatment effectiveness, effi-ciency, and alternatives. As mentioned earlier, providers could also co-ordinate information collection better and be made to use it in a more binding fashion (see below). As for physician jurisdiction, there remains no national licensing of physicians or systematic review procedure. This stems from the provincial framework and could lead to concerns including labour rigidity between provinces and regulatory duplication.

Physician reimbursement initiatives are already being established – generally taking the form of service-fee adjustments to limit physicians' income growth. However, as mentioned previously, this fails to increase physicians' accountability with regard to service costs. A more binding measure, for example, would be to allocate a fixed per-capita budget to physicians, albeit with possible refinements for population characteristics in each region (see above). This would shift the responsibility for the allocating expenditure onto physicians, enhancing the incentives for marginal-benefit analysis. In this instance physicians maintain their autonomy with regard to treatment decisions, but now have a cost-dimension in this process. Physicians may decide to form group practices as a means of spreading the financial risk. This is in a similar mode, for example, to Health Maintenance Organisations (as in the United States) or General Practice Fund Holders (as in the United Kingdom). An intermediate step is to compare physicians' per-patient (or per-treatment) expenditure more formally as a form of discipline (see Annex). However, such activities would again prove more binding in the case of a global physician budgets or capitation payments.

Enhancing market-mechanisms within the *hospital system* is also central to overall cost-containment. Within hospitals, controls can be put on staff numbers and salaries, capital expenditure, and methods of setting the total budget. In Canada, the focus of global budgets should remain on enforcing the budget cap, while introducing incentives to improve efficiency. For example, the introduction of internal competition between hospitals could be facilitated by transforming practitioner groups into "purchasers" of health services on behalf of their patients – similar to the "public competition" system in the United Kingdom.[39] Management control over hospitals' medical resources remains a powerful bargaining lever, with the levying of charges on physicians for its use immediately creating efficiency incentives. The responsibility of resource allocation is thus in the hands of physicians – who ultimately decide treatment type. Importantly, the market is internal, and is designed to reallocate resources within the system rather than regulate the total volume; global budgets remain. This also provides a more formal role for stakeholder participation, with local "health councils" remaining the manager of health care, determining population characteristics and deciding on needs.

The specific *provider-patient* relationship depends a lot on the type of hospital operating environment chosen, in particular the accounting framework used and the degree of competition that exists between hospitals and other health providers. For example, an innovation increasingly used internationally is an accounting and billing framework based on diagnostic related groups (DRGs); that is, allocating health costs according to the treatment-type. This framework allows for cost comparisons across treatment-types on a standardised basis, as well as acting as a potential indicator for levying charges on physicians in a "public competition" environment. It would also allow future hospital budgets to be based, for example, on the national average cost of each treatment-type, with the basic premise that if hospitals can perform the service at less (more) cost than the DRG-schedule, they retain the surplus(deficit).[40] Furthermore, such a framework facilitates the establishment of "cost-centres" within hospitals, again increasing accountability. An intermediate step, requiring less detailed information but providing similar efficiency incentives, would be to compare costs amongst uniform groups of hospitals to detect drift in individual budgets. This would at least provide funders some guidelines toward matching efficiency and load factors. Some provinces (Ontario and Alberta) are already experimenting with DRG-type accounting techniques.

A final advantage of applying DRG-type accounting methodologies is in relation to technology. Quantitative cost data based on treatment type will increase the ability to estimate and compare the marginal-benefit of capital equipment. At the least, it could provide a method for comparing competing technologies on a standardised basis, including not only life years saved, but also the impact on personnel costs and the opportunity cost of other forms of care.[41] However, an important caveat is that the implementation of a DRG-type system alone will not remove the ongoing antagonism between hospital managers – who are charged with minimising health costs – and physicians – who are charged with maximising health welfare. It should, however, provide a clearer indication of cost pressures.

With regard to data requirements, the most pressing areas where improvement is needed include establishing health indicators and illness severity indexes, comparable service indicators, human resource requirements, quality measures, environmental risks, and population characteristics. There is also a lack of data on nursing home and rehabilitation care provision outside of government, hindering decisions on the devolution of health care. However, before these gaps can be addressed, uniform coding standards – across all providers – are necessary, as well as consistent patient identifiers.

Importantly, the data must relate the efficiency and effectiveness of treatment to that of procedural costs and severity conditions. Such concerns have led to calls for the establishment of an information "clearing house" at the federal government level, using a standardised template.[42]

Concluding remarks

The above discussion indicates that there is no single solution, rather a host of measures which could be implemented to enhance efficiency. These are primarily related to increased accountability at all levels – funder, provider, and consumer. General themes include: promoting individual health responsibility, reallocating resources to their most cost-effective alternatives, re-addressing incentive structures, standardising accounting frameworks and co-ordinating information management, establishing human resource policies, and promoting research on health outcomes and delivery mechanisms. These are specified in Diagram 2.15.

The promotion of health and illness prevention should remain a prominent feature. To enhance this, continued research efforts into improved delivery mechanisms, appropriate human resource levels, the assessment of technology, and the reorganisation of resources into least-cost alternatives, all appear necessary and complementary. The transparency and accountability of health funding may also be strengthened through either the expanded use of user-charges and/or increased use of specific "health" premiums. Binding constraints on hospital budgets should be emphasised, albeit with increased focus on positive efficiency incentives, more informative accounting methodologies, and continued experimentation with managed competition.

The latter is mutually dependent on continued experimentation with physician incentive structures. There appears some scope for the introduction of "public-competition" practices. Internal competition

Diagram 2.15. **Possible features of an improved system**

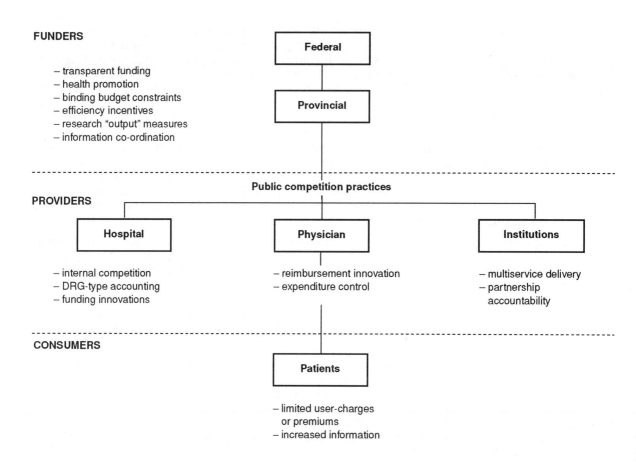

would also enhance the role of community based care, when it is the least-cost alternative. Physicians themselves should remain independent, while having a more transparent role in the policy process, and consumers should remain free to choose their practitioner. Importantly, decisions concerning the level of public resources devoted to the health sector should stay with the government, which would retain its monopoly funding position. Meanwhile, stakeholder participation could be enhanced through a more formal role for "regional" health organisations, who would become the manager – as opposed to provider – of health care.

Notes

1. Several motivations are generally cited for redressing the structure of the health system. They include: on-going variations in health status; growing waiting lists; insufficient long-term care; bottlenecks in emergency rooms; unnecessary treatment; little innovation in financing and delivery of care; and heavy reliance on institutional care. See Tanner (1993), and Champagne *et al.* (1993).

2. The 1984 Canada Health Act stems from the combination and updating of *i)* the 1957 Hospital Insurance and Diagnostics Act (HIDS) – which established a 50-50 federal-provincial cost sharing plan for hospital and diagnostic services – and *ii)* the 1966 Medical Care Act – which established a conditional cost-sharing arrangement for wider medical care services. National health insurance became the norm by 1972.

3. The latter includes native Canadians living on reserves, the military forces, prison inmates, and the Royal Canadian Mounted Police. However, the federal government is also responsible for expenditure related to health, including the Food and Drug Act, the Medical Research Council, and the National Health Research Development Programme. The Canadian Assistance Plan (CAP) also cost-shares with provinces on a wide range of health related services.

4. It reflects a strong increase in the private consumption of drugs as well as a growing elderly population who face out-of-pocket charges for long-term care. This growth can be explained, to a lesser extent, by a recent trend to de-insure some supplementary benefits.

5. Health financing through the general tax system has ensured health provision on a universal basis – with income protection guaranteed – while the portability of health insurance across provinces guarantees reasonable national access. Likewise, consumers' freedom of choice is protected through their selection of practitioner, and physicians' autonomy remains largely intact, with the majority remaining private practitioners and the professional body remaining self-regulated.

6. Prescription drug benefits exist for all seniors, as well as individuals suffering from certain chronic diseases. In most cases some form of co-payment is required from the beneficiary except from those on social welfare. However, some provinces now distinguish between seniors who do or do not receive the (federal) Guaranteed Income Support.

7. Private health insurance that duplicates services offered by public plans is not the norm, but it is not prohibited in all provinces. Also, a trend may be emerging following Nova Scotia's and British Columbia's introduction of a policy earlier, of charging health care costs arising from automobile accidents back to automobile insurance policies.

8. These practices include adverse risk selection, market segmentation, product differentiation, discontinuity in coverage, refusals of insurance, biased information regarding costs and quality, oligopolistic behaviour, and free-rider problems (see Enthoven, 1988).

9. The degree of restraint in federal transfers to provinces has been most evident since 1988. Total provincial expenditure on health care has increased 42 per cent – which includes insured health services, provincial supplementary programmes and private expenditure – on a cumulative basis over the 4 year period 1988-92 while the federal cash transfer has risen less than 1 per cent. See Boothe and Johnston (1993).

10. Provinces and territories identify a range of revenue sources. These include health premiums (British Colombia and Alberta), payroll taxes (Quebec, Ontario, Manitoba and Newfoundland), as well as various third-party sources (*e.g.* investment income, lotteries, permits, etc.). Importantly, there remains no direct relationship between health premium revenues and any individual's access to health coverage.

11. Taxes on income are generally less regressive – especially in the case of a fixed health levy – with all residents within the same income bracket paying an equivalent percentage of their income (albeit different absolute amounts); they do not discriminate according to individual health needs since they are related to income not health risk; and they imply a smaller redistribution of income than a private profit making system, with those unable to afford care protected and income security maintained.

12. Prior to the implementation of the EPF, the HIDS legislation enabled provinces to impose user-charges, although federal transfers were reduced on a dollar-for-dollar basis as a disincentive. The switch to block funding under the EPF in 1977 removed provisions for deductions. The resulting increase in user changes was seen as a threat to universality, and prompted the introduction of the Canada Health Act (1984). The Act

contains an enforcement mechanism, involving mandatory financial penalties, designed to discourage patient user-charges.

13. Even in the eventuality of zero cash under EPF, legislation provides that other federal transfers can be withheld or reduced in order to promote compliance with the Canada Health Act.

14. Approximately 85 per cent of all physicians receive a percentage of their income as fee-for-service payments, representing 65 per cent of their total professional earnings.

15. *Health Care Systems in Transition*, OECD, 1990, Table 3, p. 22.

16. Health expenditures in the United States are more than one-third higher than would be predicted by a simple linear income-expenditure relationship.

17. Mechanical extrapolations of health expenditure indicate that the ageing population *per se* is not a major factor in rising health expenditure. Instead, resource use intensity is the major cost concern with regards to care for the elderly. See Marzouk (1991) and Department of Finance (May 1992).

18. The extent to which the shift to a single-payer system resulted in significantly lower expenditure levels remains in doubt. For example, between 1975-87 real per capita expenditure on health grew at an annual average rate of 3.5 per cent per annum, compared to 3.8 in the United States, 3.2 in the United Kingdom, and 2.9 in Germany. More recently this growth has slowed to 1.9 per cent per annum between 1987-91, compared to 5.1 in the United States, 3.1 in the United Kingdom, and 2.7 in Germany. However, this may reflect the unwillingness to exercise the expenditure control a single-payer system allows during this period, rather than the system structure itself.

19. The Patented Medicine Prices Review Board (PMPRB) (1993) estimated that 105 of Canada's 177 top-selling prescription drugs were priced above the median seven other comparable industrialised nations. This has raised questions about the effectiveness of controls on drug prices. Current guidelines restrict introductory prices of new "breakthrough" drugs to the international median price. However, there are no such restrictions for "line-extensions" (the same drug in a different form) or new drugs showing less than substantial improvement over existing products. Recent Patent Act amendments took effect in February 1993 which increase the powers of the PMPRB and allow for additional determination factors to be prescribed *via* regulation.

20. This includes only direct expenditure for the administration of provincial health plans.

21. Evidence exists for price elasticities to be higher for ambulatory care than for hospital services. See Barer (1982), "The effects of user-charges on health care costs and access", Ministry of State for Social Development, unpublished report.

22. There is no single measure of health services which covers all of the dimensions of health improvement (quality), making it difficult to assign a nominal value to welfare or production gains. Instead, the output of health services are generally proxied by selected health indicators which are comparable across individuals, time, and country. Common proxies include both life and health expectancy. The latter attempts to adjust for the "quality of life" by assessing the years of life free from major disability. Nevertheless, in the absence of quality-adjustments to health output measures, current estimates may be significantly biased downward.

23. Auer (1987), using the most "favourable" measure of hospital output, found that estimated total factor productivity declined in hospitals between 1960 and 1980.

24. Future resource allocation is largely determined by past utilisation and the existing distribution of health facilities, with little formal regard for future needs. This is highlighted by the slow response of health care providers to the needs of the growing elderly population who generally demand low intensity long-term care. The result is an increasing percentage of hospital beds utilised for long-term health care at a higher cost than non-institutional care.

25. Within total health expenditure, the government's share has increased from 43 per cent in 1960 to a peak of 77 per cent in 1975, before declining slowly to 72 per cent by 1990. Nevertheless, health expenditure as a share of total government expenditure has risen from 13.3 to 14.5 per cent between 1980 and 1991. This trend is more dramatic with regard to provincial budgets, with health expenditure accounting for 19.1 per cent of their total spending in 1991, compared to 15.8 per cent in 1980. Provincial government health expenditure now accounts for 64 per cent of total public health outlays, compared to 57 per cent in 1981.

26. Ontario, for example, is using district health councils to co-ordinate care provision, multi-service agencies to provide housing, home-care and access to long-term care, and the provincial government to provide a regulatory umbrella of quality assurance and budget control.

27. Alberta's Acute Care Funding Plan reallocates resources among hospitals on the basis of a hospital "performance index". Those hospitals able to demonstrate significant cost-advantages are rewarded with increased funding – potentially at the expense of less efficient hospitals.

28. Organisations dealing with data concerning the health sector, in addition to Statistics Canada, HMRI, CCHFA, MIS, and NPDB, include: the National Health Information Council (NHIC) – involved in establishing common terminology across all jurisdictions, and the Canadian Institute of Health Information (CIHI) – which represents a merger of the HMRI, MIS and certain of the health information functions of Health Canada and Statistics Canada. The governing body of CIHI will supersede NHIC.

29. British Colombia, Saskatchewan, Manitoba, Ontario, and Quebec, accounting for 80 per cent of the population.

30. The aim is to eliminate service duplication, establish practice guidelines, and develop health outcome measures. The proposed CAPIA works in conjunction with the PMRB, CIHI, CCOHTA, and the National Health and Welfare's drug directorate.

31. For example, the Ontario provincial authorities − where one in four of the population currently receive drug subsidies − are planning changes related to prescription guidelines, eligibility requirements, drug information, reimbursement techniques, and co-ordinating pharmacists through computer links. Drug control is also being undertaken, including: reassessing the effectiveness of drugs on their scheme, only allowing replacement drugs to enter the schedule, placing a reimbursement ceiling on generic substitutes, introducing aggregate price controls, differentiating dispensing fees, and increasing expenditure on prevention and promotion.

32. Since patients with relatively low-intensity care are those most suitable for non-institutional treatment, and assuming the vacated bed is not suppressed, they will be replaced by patients in need of relatively more-intensive care. A more general result is that cost-savings will appear only in the medium term.

33. For example, real per capita health expenditure grew 0.7 per cent in 1991 compared to 3.7 per cent in 1986, and has subsequently remained subdued.

34. A general consensus is that there appears a role for the private sector in the delivery and operation of ancillary services (e.g. diagnostic laboratories) but not in the delivery of direct patient care.

35. Such changes have the ability to improve the equity of the health system, by better equalising health status as opposed to the access to or utilisation of care. For such a system to be manageable, health care costs would need to be relatively predictable by region and require a stable function of the communities characteristics. Moreover, the formula should be applicable to all communities, administratively feasible, and resistant to stakeholder manipulation (see Birch et al., 1993).

36. Corporate sector practices include, for example: management techniques, cost and profit centres, detailed accounting techniques, and increased accountability amongst managers for resource allocation. The underlying rationale for these measures is the division of tasks between professional managers − who are responsible for economising resources − and physicians − who remain responsible for patient care.

37. Both Canadian and international empirical studies of user-charges support many of these points. General results include only a small decline in consumption following the introduction of charges, with most of that decline coming from the lower income groups. See Enterline et al. (1973), Beck (1974), Beck and Horne (1980), and Barer et al. (1979).

38. Quebec, for example, levies a 3.2 per cent wage premium for health insurance, with private complementary health insurance providing between another 1 to 4 per cent to the total wage bill.

39. "Public competition" models rely on consumer preferences to ensure allocative efficiencies. Physicians compete for patient loyalty, within a given budget and often within a defined geographical location. Payment is generally on a capitation basis, with physicians retaining the freedom to allocate the resources. The difference between this and the US HMO-type system is that the consumer chooses the service, as opposed to the insurer, directly. "Mixed market" models, in contrast, rely on a mixture of private/public provision with a third party purchaser of health. For example, a district health council is charged with allocating the regional budget − potentially population adjusted − across all providers. Some potential problems in this system include increased administration costs, indirect consumer signals, and a concern that only those services providing obvious short-term outcomes will be supplied − hampering investment in prevention and promotion.

40. The system can be further refined to avoid some of the potential drawbacks − such as case-mix manipulation toward more profitable operations − by adding a case-severity index to the DRG. This would ensure that hospitals who deal with more severe cases, needing more inputs, will not be financially disadvantaged.

41. Cost-benefit analysis estimated on the basis of, for example, the potential gain in life years could act as a starting point for managerial decisions of capital equipment usage. Data for each DRG, severity-index, and age group could be used in the analysis. Added to this could be some form of "quality of life" adjustment, as suitable information becomes available.

42. See National Health Information Council (1991).

Bibliography

Angus, D.E. (1991), "Review of Significant Health Care Commissions and Task Forces in Canada Since 1983-84", Canadian Hospital Association, Medical Association and Nurses Association, Ottawa.

Angus, D.E. (1993), "Health Care Cost-Effectiveness in Canada", Queens University of Ottawa, Economic Prospects.

Auer, L. (1987), "Canadian Hospital Costs and Productivity", a study prepared for the Economic Council of Canada, Ottawa.

Barer, M.L., R.G. Evans and G.L. Stoddart (1979), "Controlling Health Care Costs by Direct Charges to Patients: Snare or Delusion?", *Ontario Economic Council Occasional Paper*, No. 10.

Barer, M.L. and G.L. Stoddart (1991), "Toward Integrated Medical Resource Policies for Canada", Report prepared for the Federal/Provincial/Territorial Conference of Deputy Ministers of Health, Canada, June.

Beck, R.G. (1974), "The Effect of Copayment on the Poor", *Journal of Human Resources*, 9, pp. 129-142.

Beck, R.G. and J.M. Horne (1976), "Economic Class and Risk Avoidance", *Journal of Risk Insurance*, No. 75.

Beck, R.G. and J.M. Horne (1980), "Utilisation of Publicly Insured Health Services in Saskatchewan Before, During, and After Copayment", *Medical Care*, No. 8, pp. 787-806.

Birch, S., J. Eyles, J. Hurley, B. Hutchison and S. Chambers (1993), "A Needs-Based Approach to Resource Allocation in Health Care", *Canadian Public Policy*, XIX:1, pp. 68-85.

Blendon, R.J. *et al.* (1993), "Physicians' Perspectives on Caring for Patients in the United States, Canada, and West Germany", *The New England Journal of Medicine*, Vol. 328, No. 14, April.

Boothe, P. and B. Johnson (1993), "Stealing the Emperor's Clothes: Deficit Offloading and National Standards in Health Care", *C.D. Howe Institute Commentary*, No. 41, March.

Boyle, P., R. Pineault and D. Roberge (1992), "Assessing Quebec's Multi-Component Program to Reduce Emergency Room Overcrowding", *Canadian Public Policy*, XVIII:2, pp. 189-202.

Champagne, F., A-P. Contandriopoulos, J. Denis, A. Lemay and R. Pineault (1993), "Options for Health System Regulation: The Case of the Quebec Health Care Reform", University of Montreal, Canada.

Champagne, F., A-P. Contandriopoulos, A. Preker and A. Lemay (1991), "Évolution et projections des dépenses socio-sanitaires au Québec", Université de Montréal.

Culyer, A.J. (1989), "Health Care Expenditures in Canada: Myth and Reality; Past and Future", *Canadian Tax Paper*, No. 82, January.

Danzon, P.M. (1992), "Hidden Overhead Costs: Is Canada's System Really Less Expensive?", *Health Affairs*.

Department of Finance (1991), "Factors Underlying the Upward Pressure on Expenditures in the Canada Health Care Sector", *Economic Studies and Policy Analysis*, September.

Department of Finance (1992), "Federal-Provincial Study on the Cost of Government and Expenditure Management", Ottawa, May.

Enterline, S., McDonald and McDonald (1973), "Effects of 'Free' Medical Care on Medical Practice: The Quebec Experience", *The New England Journal of Medicine*, 31 May.

Enthoven, A.C. (1988), "Theory and Practice of Managed Competition in Health Care Finance", *Lectures in Economics*, Vol. 9.

Enthoven, A. and R. Kronick (1989), "A Consumer-Choice Health Plan for the 1990s: Universal Health Insurance in a System Designed to Promote Quality and Economy", *The New England Journal of Medicine*.

Epp, J. (1986), "Achieving Health for All: A Framework for Health Promotion", Ministry of National Health and Welfare, Ottawa, Canada, November.

Evans, R.G. and M.L. Barer (1989), "Controlling Health Expenditures: The Canadian Reality", *The New England Journal of Medicine*, Vol. 320, No. 9.

Evans, R.G., M.L. Barer, C. Hertzman, G.M. Anderson, I.R. Pulcins and J. Lomas (1989), "The Long Good-Bye: The Great Transformation of the British Columbia Hospital System", *Health Services Research*, 24:4, October.

Evans, R.G. (1990), "Tension, Compression, and Shear: Directions, Stresses and Outcomes of Health Care Cost Control", *Journal of Health Politics, Policy and Law*, Vol. 15, No. 1, Spring.

Federal/Provincial Taskforce (1992), "A Canadian Agency for Pharmaceutical Information Assessment (National Formulary Service)", Report to the Conference of Deputy Ministers of Health, 4 December.

Feeny, D. and G. Stoddart (1988), "Toward Improved Health Technology Policy in Canada: A Proposal for the National Health Technology Assessment Council", *CHEPA Working Paper Series*, No. 4, May.

Ferguson, B. (1993*a*), "Factors Affecting Expenditure on Physicians Services in Canada: A Cointegration Analysis", Queens University of Ottawa, Economic Projects and Department of Economics, University of Guelph.

Ferguson, B. (1993*b*), "Supplier-Induced Demand: Dynamic Modelling", Queens University of Ottawa, Economic Projects and Department of Economics, University of Guelph.

Fournier, M-A. and A-P. Contandriopoulos (1992), "La projection de l'offre de services médicaux au Québec entre 1990 and 2020", Université de Montréal.

Glennerster, H., M. Matsaganis and P. Owens (1991), "A Foothold for Funding", *King's Fund Institute Research Report*, No. 12.

Glennerster, H. and M. Matsaganis (1992), "The English and Swedish Health Care Reforms", The Welfare State Programme Suntory-Toyota International Centre for Economics and Related Disciplines, *Discussion Paper*, No. WSP/79, November.

Gorechi, P. K. (1992), "Controlling Drug Expenditure in Canada: The Ontario Experience", Economic Council of Canada and the Ontario Ministry of Health.

Gouvernement du Québec (1990), "Une réforme axée sur le citoyen", ministère de la Santé et des Services sociaux.

Government of Canada (1991), *Building Partnerships*, government response to the Standing Committee Report entitled "The Health Care System in Canada and its Funding: No Easy Solutions", November.

Grogan, C.M. (1992), "Deciding on Access and Levels of Care: A Comparison of Canada, Britain, Germany and the United States", *Journal of Health Politics, Policy and Law*, Vol. 17, No. 2, Summer.

Health and Welfare Canada (1992), "A Profile for Practising Physicians in Canada from the National Physician Database, 1989-90", Health Information Division.

Health and Welfare Canada (1993), *Fact Sheets*, March.

Hurley, J. and N.A. Johnson (1991), "The Effects of Co-payments Within Drug Reimbursement Programs", *Canadian Public Policy*, XVII:4, pp. 473-489.

Iglehart, J.K. (1986), "Canada's Health Care System", in Health Policy Report, *The New England Journal of Medicine*.

Krasny, J. and I.R. Ferrier (1990), "The Canadian Healthcare System in Perspective", Bogart, Delafield, Ferrier Inc., Morristown, Canada, July.

Lalonde, M. (1974), "A New Perspective on the Health of Canadians", Health and Welfare Canada, Ottawa, Canada.

MacKenzie, M.D., B. Tholl and G. Brimacombe (1992), "Physician Compensation in Canada: The Economics of Balancing Patient, Provider and Payer Interests", Queens University, Canada, December.

Marzouk, M.S. (1991), "Aging, Age-Specific Health Care Costs and the Future Health Care Burden in Canada", *Canadian Public Policy*, XVII:4, pp. 490-506.

Mechanic, D. (1991), "Changing Our Health Care System", *Medical Care Review*, 48:3, Autumn.

Ministry of Health (1993), "Managing Health Care Resources" 1993/1994, Ontario Provincial Government.

Ministry of Health, Ministry of Community and Social Services, Ministry of Citizenship (1993), "A Policy Framework", *Partnerships in Long-Term Care: A New Way to Plan, Manage and Deliver Services and Community Support*, Ontario Provincial Government, April.

Ministry of Health, Ministry of Community and Social Services, Ministry of Citizenship (1993), "A Local Planning Framework", *Building Partnerships in Long-Term Care: A New Way to Plan, Manage and Deliver Services and Community Support*, Ontario Provincial Government, May.

Muldoon, J.M. and G.L. Stoddart (1992), "Publicly Financed Competition in Health Care Delivery: A Canadian Simulation Model", *Centre for Health Economics and Policy Analysis Working Paper Series*, No. 14.

National Health Information Council (1991), "Health Information for Canada: Report of the National Task Force on Health Information", Ottawa.

National Union (1993), "Restructuring of Our Health Care System: A Review of the Changes Taking Place in the Health Care Sector in the Provinces of Canada", *Research Study*, Draft No. 4, May.

O'Brecht, M. and J. Doutriaux (1992), "Impact of Private Non-Profit Sector on the Distribution of Canadian Health Research Funding", *Canadian Public Policy*, XVIII:3, pp. 290-299.

OECD (1987), *Financing and Delivering Health Care: A Comparative Analysis of OECD Countries*, Paris.

OECD (1988), "The Future of Social Protection", *Social Policy Studies*, No. 6, Paris.

OECD (1991), "Market-type Mechanisms and Health Services in the UK", by H. Wennester, *Occasional Paper No. 2*, PUMA, Paris.

OECD (1992a), *Progress in Structural Reform: An Overview*, Paris.

OECD (1992b), "US Health Care at the Crossroads", *Health Policy Studies*, No. 1, Paris.

OECD (1992c), "The Reform of Health Care: A Comparative Analysis of Seven OECD Countries", *Health Policy Studies*, No. 2, Paris.

OECD (1993a), "OECD Health Systems: Facts and Trends 1960-1991", *Health Policy Studies*, No. 3, Vol. II and II, Paris.

OECD (1993b), "Market-type Mechanisms and Hospital Regulation: Belgium, France, Germany and the United Kingdom", by D. Fixari, J-C. Moisdon, D. Tonneau, *Occasional Papers*, PUMA, Paris.

OECD (1994), *The Reform of Health Care Systems: A Review of Seventeen OECD Countries*, Paris.

Porter, B. (1991), "The Health Care System in Canada and its Funding: No Easy Solution", *First Report on the Standing Committee on Health and Welfare, Social Affairs, and the Status of Women,* House of Commons, Canada.

Rachlis, M. and C. Kushner (1989), "Second Opinion: What's Wrong with Canada's Health Care System and How to Fix It", Toronto.

Redelmeier, D.A. and V.R. Fuchs (1993), "Hospital Expenditures in the United States and Canada", *The New England Journal of Medicine,,* March.

Rochaix, L. and C. Largeron (1989), "Facteurs économiques et pratique médicale au Québec: vers un budget global en ambulatoire", *Sciences Sociales et Santé*, Vol. VII, No. 2.

Sakala, C. (1990), "The Development of National Medical Care Programs in the United Kingdom and Canada: Applicability to Current Conditions in the United States", *Journal of Health Politics, Policy and Law*, Vol. 15, No. 4, Winter.

Statistics Canada, *Medical Care Data Base.*

Summary of the Report of the British Columbia Royal Commission on Health Care and Costs (1991), "Closer to Home".

Tanner, M. (1993), "How Not to Fix the Health Care Crisis", *Business Economics*, April.

Weisbrod, B.A. (1991), "The Health Care Quadrilemma: An Essay on Technological Change, Insurance, Quality of Care, and Cost Containment", *Journal of Economic Literature*, Vol. XXIX, June, pp. 523-552.

Annex

Health care commitments and cost-containment efforts across Canadian provinces in the 1970s and 1980s

The Canadian health system consists of twelve independent jurisdictions, each responsible for providing necessary health care on a universal basis. Although these jurisdictions (ten provinces and two territories) operate under the federal umbrella of the 1984 Canadian Health Act, variations in the method of health provision exist, leading to differences in both the levels and growth rates of per capita health expenditure. This annex briefly outlines the major trends in health spending across provinces and reviews recent provincial cost-containment measures. With regard to the latter, an emphasis is placed on Quebec, where despite its relatively high level of health expenditure – both as a per cent of GDP and total public expenditure – cost-control reforms commenced earlier and have generally been more thorough with regard to constraining physician remuneration. This is not to deny that, as is common across all provinces, the Quebec health system continues to experience financial strains.

Provincial health expenditure and resources

Expenditure trends

Since 1975, following the gradual implementation of universal basic health-care, health expenditure as a share of GDP has grown in all provinces (Table A1)*. This growth has not been uniform however and has resulted in a general convergence of the expenditure-to-GDP ratios across provinces. As regards the three most populated provinces – Quebec, Ontario and British Columbia (which account for over 70 per cent of total population) – Quebec experienced the smallest increase.

Per capita health expenditures across provinces are closely related to per capita income (Diagram A1), and this relation explains a large proportion of the variation in health expenditure across provinces. Health expenditure

Table A.1. **Provincial health expenditure as a share of GDP**

Provinces	Population 1987 (thousands)	1975	1987
Newfoundland	568.1	10.7	11.7
Prince Edward Island	127.3	12.0	12.2
Nova Scotia	878.0	10.1	11.6
New Brunswick	712.3	8.8	10.8
Quebec	6 592.6	8.0	8.9
Ontario	9 265.0	6.7	8.2
Manitoba	1 079.0	7.9	10.0
Saskatchewan	1 015.8	6.7	11.0
Alberta	2 377.7	5.5	7.7
British Colombia	2 925.0	7.1	8.9
Canada	25 617.3	7.3	8.7

Source: Health and Welfare Canada.

---

* The provincial data on health expenditure available at the time this survey was orginally prepared was 1987. Since preliminary data covering the period 1987-91 have been released, the provincial trends analysed in this annex through 1987 apply to the more recent years.

Diagram A1. **Per capita health expenditure by province, 1987**

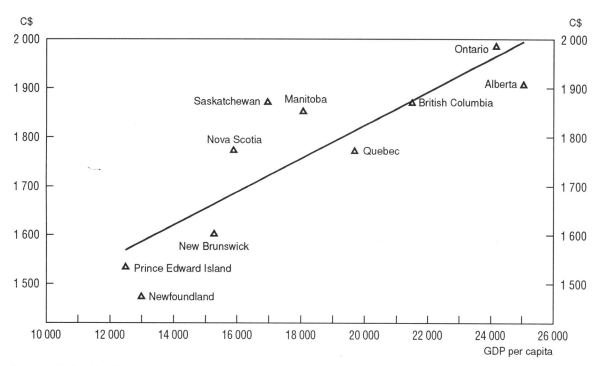

Source: "National health expenditures in Canada, 1975-1987", *Canadian Economic Observer.*

Table A.2. **Per capita health expenditure**

In dollars

Provinces	1978	Percentage growth per annum 1978 to 1987	1987
Newfoundland	615	10.2	1 473
Prince Edward Island	631	10.3	1 533
Nova Scotia	635	12.1	1 772
New Brunswick	578	11.9	1 601
Quebec	737	10.2	1 770
Ontario	743	11.5	1 985
Manitoba	739	10.7	1 852
Saskatchewan	692	11.7	1 871
Alberta	736	11.1	1 906
British Columbia	800	9.9	1 869
Canada	733	10.9	1 869

Source: "National health expenditure in Canada 1975-1987", *Canadian Economic Observer.*

in Saskatchewan, Manitoba and Nova Scotia remains above that predicted by their per capita income (as indicated by the regression line) while Ontario and British Columbia are close to it.

In 1978 health expenditure per capita in the three most populated provinces was in all cases above the national average (Table A2). However, since then, both British Columbia and Quebec have experienced a below average growth rate. Per capita health expenditure grew faster than the national average in Ontario throughout this period, and remains the highest of all provinces. Again, this is largely explained by its relatively rapid per capita income growth.

Table A.3. **Structure of health expenditure**

Provinces	Expenditure per capita 1991	Percentage of total health expenditure							
		Hospitals		Other institutions		Professional services		Drugs	
		1975	1991	1975	1991	1975	1991	1975	1991
Newfoundland	2 107	48.5	43.6	7.7	11.6	13.6	13.7	10.2	20.0
Prince Edward Island	2 140	44.3	38.6	14.7	14.9	17.3	15.5	11.8	19.3
Nova Scotia	2 248	48.1	44.3	6.1	8.6	19.1	17.5	11.4	17.0
New Brunswick	2 107	49.9	41.9	7.1	10.2	16.2	15.8	10.2	16.4
Quebec	2 282	48.7	42.5	8.1	11.7	19.5	17.8	9.5	13.3
Ontario	2 511	42.4	36.7	12.3	9.1	23.1	25.8	11.3	14.4
Manitoba	2 373	44.9	38.7	14.8	12.6	18.3	16.8	10.6	10.7
Saskatchewan	2 454	40.6	34.0	13.3	17.6	17.4	16.0	13.4	12.6
Alberta	2 288	43.0	40.4	11.8	7.2	22.1	23.1	10.2	12.6
British Columbia	2 412	39.9	34.3	8.8	10.4	28.1	24.7	11.0	17.5

Note: Hospitals: services provided by hospitals;
Other institutions: services provided by other medical institutions, home care and ambulances;
Professional services: services provided by physicians, dentists and other professionals;
Drugs: expenditures for drugs.
The total includes other expenditure such as eye glasses, hearing aids and prostheses.
The 1991 estimates were not available at the time this survey was originally published with 1987 figures.
Source: "National health expenditures in Canada 1975-1987", *Canadian Economic Observer* and *Preliminary estimates of health expenditure in Canada*, Provincial/Territorial summary report 1987-1991.

Table A.4. **Public spending on health**

Provinces	As a share of total health expenditure		Provincial government health expenditure as a share of total provincial expenditure	
	1975	1987	1980/81	1991/92
Newfoundland	76.4	74.2	18.3	22.7
Prince Edward Island	78.4	75.9	18.2	19.8
Nova Scotia	77.4	70.9	23.4	28.0
New Brunswick	78.2	76.1	22.4	23.4
Quebec	81.0	77.2	22.0	22.9
Ontario	73.4	70.5	27.0	30.2
Manitoba	78.1	76.4	26.9	25.2
Saskatchewan	72.2	76.2	21.7	23.6
Alberta	76.8	79.2	22.8	25.2
British Columbia	72.6	72.5	29.1	28.4

Source: Health and Welfare Canada.

Despite drugs being the fastest growing component of health expenditure, hospitals still account for the majority of expenditure across all provinces (Table A3). Since 1975 all provinces have reduced the proportion of health-expenditure devoted to hospital services, reflecting their desire to increase community-based non-institutional health care. Another notable feature has been the relatively subdued growth in expenditure on professional services in several provinces since 1975. Quebec experienced the largest decline in the proportion of expenditure devoted to medical professionals, reflecting earlier and relatively more stringent controls on physician remuneration in that province (see below).

The share of public health expenditure in total health expenditure decreased across all provinces (except Saskatchewan and Alberta) between 1975 and 1987 (Table A4). Ontario has the lowest public share, while Quebec, although experiencing a large decline since the mid-1970s, continues to have the highest. The share of public health spending as a percentage of total public expenditure increased across all provinces except Manitoba and British Columbia during the 1980s. Throughout this period federal contributions to provincial budgets grew at a slower rate than that of provincial health expenditure (Diagram A2). The level of these federal transfers are not linked to provincial spending trends, being instead a block fund.

Diagram A2.   EPF[1] transfers for health
Annual percentage change

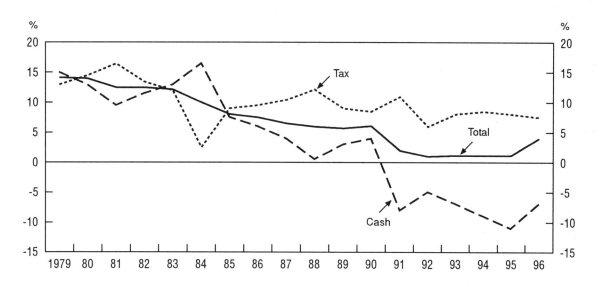

1. EPF: Established Programmes Financing, as detailed in the Federal-Provincial Fiscal Arrangements and Federal Post-Secondary Education and Health Contributions Act (1977).

Source : "The Health Care System in Canada and its Funding: no easy solution", Report of the Standing Committee on Health and Welfare, B. Porter, Chairman, House of Commons, Canada.

Health resources

The more populated provinces generally have fewer short-term beds per 1 000 population than the national average (Table A5). Some factors which help explain this difference between provinces includes the need for smaller provinces to maintain a minimum level of beds by major medical speciality (diseconomies of scale), the long distance that many inhabitants of the Prairies and the Atlantic provinces (the more sparsely populated regions) have to travel to reach services, and the higher proportion of the elderly in some provinces. Quebec, for example, has a relatively young population (10.9 per cent of persons aged 65 or over) compared to Saskatchewan (13.6 per cent of persons aged 65 and over) implying less demand for hospital care. However, the pattern of bed availability across provinces is generally not reflected in per capita hospital expenditure. This can be partially explained by differences in the intensity of health care provided (proxied by the ratio of physicians per capita) as well as differences in the average length-of-stay in hospitals (Table A5). That is, hospital expenditure is more correlated with the number of admissions as opposed to beds. The three most populated provinces have a per capita physician supply higher than the national average, with a positive correlation between the number of physicians per capita and the prevailing level of per capita health expenditure.

In summary, provincial health expenditure has risen almost uniformly – albeit at varying rates – with respect to population, GDP, and total public expenditure. This has led to a general trend across provinces towards health-spending containment as briefly outlined below.

Provincial cost-containment policies

Managing global budgets

Since the mid-1970s all provinces have modified the way hospitals are financed, progressively replacing line-by-line budgeting techniques with prospective global budgets. In principle, this monopoly-funding position of provincial governments implies that a cost-containment policy should be very effective. However, given that any expenditure constraint must also be consistent with the principles of the Health Act, the actual enforcement of budget caps has been made difficult. This is especially so when it implies service rationing and/or queuing in the

Table A.5. **Health care resources**

Provinces	Active civilian physicians per 100 000 population	Number of beds (short-term non-psychiatric hospitals) per 100 000 population	Length of stay (number of days)
	1992	1988-89	1987
Newfoundland	155	4.72	9.0
Prince Edward Island	132	5.12	7.1
Nova Scotia	193	5.44	10.2
New Brunswick	140	5.03	10.8
Quebec	209	3.76	12.3
Ontario	200	3.75	10.1
Manitoba	181	4.73	9.4
Saskatchewan	151	6.54	8.7
Alberta	172	4.49	8.4
British Columbia	207	3.60	12.3
Yukon	131	4.20	
North West Territories	107	2.22	
Canada	195	4.07	10.4

Source: Health and Welfare Canada.

absence of offsetting efficiency gains. Nevertheless, global budgets have generally been enforced more rigidly since the mid-1980s with, for example, projected real declines in health expenditure in Ontario's 1993/94 budget.

Raising price awareness

Implementing user charges

During the early 1980s, in response to demands from their populations, provinces progressively increased the coverage of health-services provided. These included, for example, dental programs for children and wider drug plans for the elderly and welfare recipients. However, during the latter half of the 1980s this trend reversed. Indeed, many provinces are now undertaking, or at least contemplating, the expansion of user charges and the de-insurance of certain complementary health-services (*i.e.* optometry and curative dental services). All provinces currently implement some form of user-charge, predominantly on pharmaceuticals, although these remain low when compared internationally and often limited to specific population groups (*i.e.* low income groups and the elderly are usually exempt). Nevertheless Quebec, Nova Scotia, New Brunswick, and Saskatchewan have all recently increased user charges. These generally take the form of small co-payments on prescription charges for elderly patients who had previously been exempt. Nominal charges for certain non-necessary hospital visits have also appeared as well as more stringent monitoring of reimbursement for services.

Levying specific health taxes

Another method of increasing cost-awareness concerns the transparency of health-funding. In general provinces fund their health-systems from general tax revenues. This eliminates the link between individual health care consumption and payment, thereby lowering the cost-awareness of consumers. Raising taxes through specific tax contributions has been increasingly used in provinces as a means to partially restoring this link – albeit in a less direct fashion than user charges. Seven provinces currently implement some form of health levy, with this accounting for over 50 per cent of health revenue in New Brunswick and Nova Scotia in 1991. Likewise, Quebec levies a specific health insurance contribution on employers equal to 3.75 per cent of the payroll, which funds one-third of the public health budget. Alberta and British Columbia likewise levy health premiums as part funding of their health expenditure, although these generally account for a lower proportion of total revenue. Nevertheless, Alberta has stated intentions to fund at least 50 per cent of its public health from this source in the near future.

Controlling physician's remuneration: the case of Quebec

In Quebec, as in other provinces, physicians are free to remain outside the public health-system although there is little incentive to do so. Indeed, 99 per cent of Quebec's physicians participate in the provincial system. This implies working on a fee-for-services basis and submitting remuneration claims to the "Régie d'assurance-maladie du Québec" (RAMQ), the government monopoly-payer. As in other provinces, physicians have the moral incentive to provide the best treatment possible, with this promoted financially by the fee-for-service payment methodology.

However, this combination of factors appears to have led to supply-induced demand – and associated cost increases – further compounded by the ongoing growth in the physician population.

In direct response to these cost-pressures, the Quebec authorities significantly enhanced control over physician remuneration through the introduction of collective and individual income caps. Under the 1976 agreement between the Quebec government and the medical associations, fee schedules are negotiated between the provincial government and the two physician associations (representing general practitioners and specialists), establishing an average target earnings figure for the forthcoming year. This is based on the current year's target where, if effective income growth this year is above target, next year's objective is reduced by the amount of this overrun.

Nevertheless, since such fee schedules do not control the quantity or the nature of services provided, the Quebec authorities imposed further individual remuneration controls. A quarterly ceiling on gross billings has been established for individual general practitioners (with specific exemptions for physicians working in remote areas). Billings in excess of this ceiling are subsequently reimbursed at only 25 per cent of the fee schedule. Such action does not exist for specialists however, given the concerns regarding their availability, notably outside the Montreal metropolitan area. Instead, specialists are monitored by both their professional associations and the "Régie d'assurance-maladie du Québec" (RAMQ). The latter organisation compares the practice of both generalists and specialists, submitting individual cases to a peer review committee. This overcomes the problem of asymmetry of medical-expertise since the physician whose practice significantly differs from the average is examined before a "comité de révision" which is composed of medical experts. The committee can issue recommendations, ask the physician to reimburse part of the fees received, or suppress the payment of fees. More generally, the RAMQ also issues recommendations and provides information on drug prescriptions on a collective basis.

To date the control of physicians' fees has proved to be effective, with no significant gap existing between target and actual income. Success is also reflected in the declining share of total health expenditure devoted to professional services (see above). Furthermore, the ceiling imposed on physicians' fees has not prevented the ratio of physicians' net income to average industrial worker compensation from rising (from 3.34 in 1983 to 3.94 in 1991). These trends have subsequently prompted other provinces (Newfoundland, Nova Scotia, Prince Edward Island and Ontario) to implement some form of individual remuneration capping. However, in the case of Quebec, since physicians' fee-negotiations concern the evolution in average physician incomes and not a global budget, increasing physician numbers still imply ongoing cost-pressures. The number of physicians in Quebec grew at an average annual rate of 3.4 per cent during the 1980s, near the 3.2 per cent growth in Canada as a whole, and well in excess of the 0.7 per cent average annual growth in Quebec's population. However, throughout this period the number of medical students has declined substantially (from 586 in 1982 to 481 in 1987), although this will be effective in reducing the physician-population ratio only in the medium term.

To sum up, provincial health expenditure has risen in all provinces, implying increased demands on tax revenues. This has led to ongoing efforts to contain costs and enhance the efficiency of the health sector. However, it appears that no single province has succeeded in providing a complete solution, albeit with some positive examples existing. These include, most notably, Quebec's effort with regard to physician salaries, the agreement across all provinces concerning physician numbers, and a general trend towards raising price awareness through the use of health levies and health-specific taxes.

Chapter 3

ICELAND

As in most other OECD countries, Iceland's system of health care has become a subject of preoccupation in recent years. While the public is largely satisfied with both the accessibility and the quality of care it receives,[1] the authorities are increasingly concerned with the expense of operating a largely open-ended and free system, especially in the context of economic stagnation which afflicted the country in the past six years. While many of the problems faced by the system are to be found in other OECD countries, Iceland is confronted with several which are peculiar to its situation: a very small and fairly isolated country whose population is largely confined to the capital region, with the remainder rather remotely located.

While there is room for improvement in some aspects of the health-care system, it is fairly efficient in delivering high-quality care to the entire population at an overall cost which is only modestly above the average of OECD countries. Nevertheless, over the longer term, certain immutable traits of the demand for health care services, in particular the tendency for demand to grow more than proportionally with income will make it increasingly difficult to finance their provision without changing the system by introducing elements of competition among providers and relying to a greater extent on user-pay measures or even by imposing a global budget constraint.

Overview of the health care system

Many of the characteristics of the Icelandic health care system are shared with other Nordic countries. All residents are covered by public health insurance as determined by the 1971 Act on social security. About 87 per cent of total medical billings are paid by the public purse, a share that had been gradually rising until the late 1970s, but which has been declining since 1984. While hospital treatment is free, patients face co-payments for most ambulatory care, as well as for pharmaceuticals. The delivery of care is rather decentralised − local communities participate through a system of municipal health boards − but the role of central government in the planning and co-ordination functions is relatively strong. In 1990, primary health care was further centralised, with the State taking over complete financial responsibility in this domain, but a return of some functions, for example nursing-home care, to the municipalities is a possibility. Ambulatory care is provided in out-patient clinics in major hospitals and by privately practising specialists. Primary health care is mainly provided by a network of some 70 public health centres,[2] but these are supplemented by private general practitioners in the capital area.

Despite its population of some 260 000, there are some 25 hospital units in Iceland, but only a few are of substantial size. 62 per cent of hospital beds are in the public sector (about half are administered by the State and half by local authorities), with the remainder catering primarily to the needs of the elderly, handicapped and alcoholics and others in need of rehabilitation. Even in a small country such as Iceland, there is a problem of regional distribution of hospital services: occupancy rates are low in many of the frequently more modern hospitals located outside the Reykjavik area, at the same time as the capital's three main hospitals are faced with excess demand and waiting lists for some procedures.

As intimated above, Iceland has an unusually high proportion of hospital beds given over to chronic care of the elderly. Indeed, nearly twice as many as in other Nordic nations of those over the age of 65 are institutionalised (Table 3.1). This appears to be due to insufficient recourse to home health care: there is a lack of co-ordination with those providing social assistance, a responsibility of the local

Table 3.1. **Care of the elderly**

Per cent

		Iceland	Denmark	Finland	Norway	Sweden
A.	**The housing situation of those over the age of 65, 1984-91**					
	Live in own homes	87.2	91.3	92.5	89.2	91.4
	Live in institutions	9.7	5.0	6.2	6.8	3.0
	Live in other residences for the elderly	3.1	3.7	1.3	4.0	5.6
B.	**Share of those over the age of 65 who received some home health care, 1990**	12.6	24.6	21.4	19.0	17.5

Source: Surgeon General of Iceland.

authorities.[3] The result has been a rapid rise in public expenditure on nursing-home care since 1987, despite unusually favourable demographic developments in recent years (Diagram 3.1): the share of the population aged 65 and over – 11 per cent in 1993 – is the lowest in the OECD area except Turkey. Although most other countries, including the other Nordics, were reversing the upward trend in such expenditures by the late 1970s, in Iceland no such brake has been observed.

Outcomes

Iceland has managed to turn in an enviable record of health outcomes (Table 3.2), possibly thanks to what is largely a relatively healthy diet and life style,[4] a relatively low volume of per-capita consumption of pharmaceuticals,[5] not to mention the excellent average level of training of the health-services professions as well as a systematic preference for preventive medicine.[6] For example, life expectancy at birth and at age 60 have been consistently above levels seen elsewhere, although there has been a noticeable slowdown in the trend improvement in recent years, especially for females, leading to a significant reduction in Iceland's lead. Second, the rates of infant and perinatal mortality have been well below OECD averages, although here, too, there is some evidence of catch-up by other OECD countries.[7] Finally, the incidence of premature deaths (that is before the age of 65) due to illness is low and, as elsewhere, is continuing to decline at a reasonably steady pace. The occurrence of heart disease has been successfully reduced by a factor of nearly three since 1970; however, rather less success has been had in controlling the spread of cancer.

Costs and financing

The pecuniary cost of achieving such outcomes has been high and increasing over time in Iceland as elsewhere. By 1991, total health spending reached 8.4 per cent of GDP,[8] an increase of nearly 2 percentage points in the previous decade and double the average figure recorded in the first half of the 1960s. Although there was a shift toward the public share of financing in the 1970s, this was partly reversed in the first half of the 1980s, and the private share is only about half the OECD average (Diagram 3.2). Nevertheless, the proportion of total public expenditure allocated to this function rose rather steadily from the mid-1970s, reaching a peak of over 20 per cent in 1987, well above levels seen elsewhere in the OECD. Since then, this growth has been reined in through a number of measures which will be examined in greater detail below.

Given the very high rate of inflation experienced in recent decades, the average rates of increase in health-care expenditures has been rather startling in nominal terms – 43 per cent per year between 1970 and 1990, for example (Table 3.3). However, even adjusting for average inflation in the economy, health expenditures rose some 7 per cent per year over this period. Partly, this reflects changes in relative prices: medical-care prices have increased an average of 0.8 percentage points per year faster than those than elsewhere in the economy. However, growth in the volume of care provided of some 6 per cent per year accounts for the bulk of the growth of health-care spending in excess of average

Diagram 3.1. Public expenditure on nursing-home care
1980 = 100

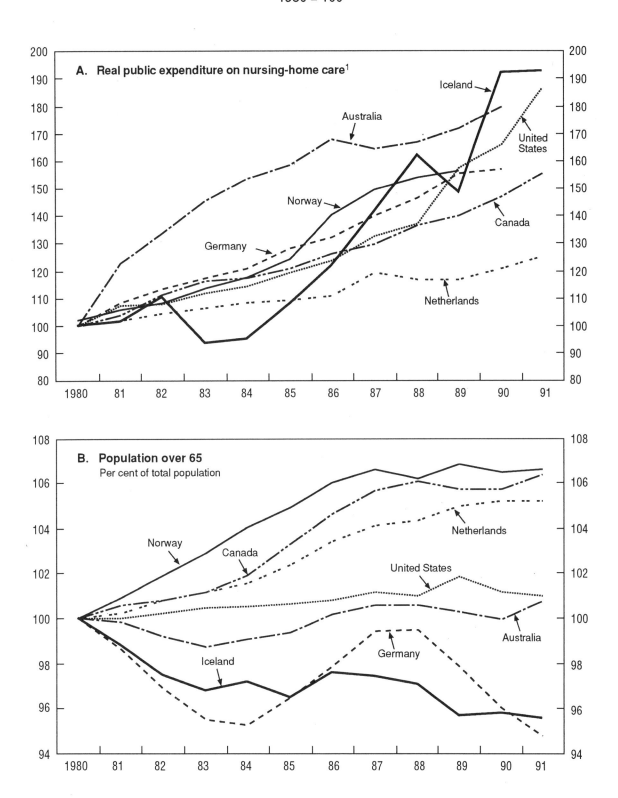

A. Real public expenditure on nursing-home care[1]

Iceland

Australia

United States

Norway

Canada

Germany

Netherlands

B. Population over 65
Per cent of total population

Norway

Canada

Netherlands

United States

Australia

Iceland

Germany

1. Using the GDP deflator.
Source: OECD (1993), *OECD Health System: Facts and Trends, 1960-1991.*

Table 3.2. **Comparative health outcomes**

		1960	1973	1980	1985	1990
A. Life expectancy						
Iceland						
Life expectancy at birth	– Male	70.7	71.6	73.7	74.7	75.7
	– Female	75.0	77.5	79.7	80.2	80.3
Life expectancy at age 60	– Male	18.6	18.6	19.4	19.5	20.0
	– Female	20.4	21.7	23.0	22.9	23.3
Simple OECD average						
Life expectancy at birth	– Male	67.9	69.2	67.8	68.9	73.1
	– Female	73.0	75.5	74.0	75.1	79.4
Life expectancy at age 60	– Male	16.3	16.4	16.3	16.8	18.3
	– Female	19.1	20.2	20.4	21.0	22.7
		1960-64	1970-74	1980-84	1985-89	1990-91
B. Perinatal and infant mortality[1]						
Iceland						
Perinatal mortality		2.3	1.8	0.8	0.7	0.5
Infant mortality		1.7	1.2	0.7	0.6	0.6
Simple OECD average						
Perinatal mortality		3.0	2.1	1.2	0.9	n.a.
Infant mortality		2.8	1.8	1.0	0.9	n.a.
		1960-64	1970-74	1980-84	1985-89	1990
C. Incidence of premature death due to illness[2]						
Iceland		50.4	38.8	25.5	22.6	20.3
Simple OECD average		69.5	52.0	35.5	31.1	n.a.

1. Per cent of live and still births and live births alone, respectively.
2. Potential years of life before age 65 lost per thousand people under the age of 65.
Source: OECD.

inflation. Population growth accounts for a bit more than 1 per cent of this, leaving an average annual increase in the volume of per capita expenditure of nearly 5 per cent. This is well above the corresponding growth rate in real per capita GDP.[9] The implied long-run average (arc) elasticity of volume expenditure with respect to real income has been of the order of 1.5, but econometric evidence presented in Annexes I and II indicates that even this estimate may be slightly lower than the true underlying value.

Several other features of the evolution of health care expenditures are worth noting. First, there has been some tendency for volumes to slow over time: the average annual volume increase over the period 1975-90 was, at 5.5 per cent, over one-third less than what had been experienced during the previous fifteen-year period. Furthermore, the slowdown has been reinforced in recent years, in line with the nation's overall economic stagnation, as health care volumes have not increased since 1988. Second, superimposed on this decelerating trend has been a stabilisation in relative prices in the 1980s, although during the latter half of the decade the relative price of dental care moved up strongly. Third, spending pressures have been especially strong in dental services, pharmaceutical consumption[10] and nursing and convalescence homes (13.8 per cent of the total in 1991, compared to 8.5 per cent in 1980), while it has been the costs of hospital inpatient care which have slowed most noticeably during the 1980s (Diagram 3.3). This was indeed a necessary improvement, given that like other Nordic countries, Iceland has a very high share of aggregate health care expenditures allocated to inpatient care.

An international comparison

Iceland spent the equivalent of $1 457 (in purchasing-power-parity terms) per person in 1991 on health care, the eighth highest in the OECD countries, compared with its tenth place in the per capita

Diagram 3.2. **Total expenditure on health, 1970-91**

Left scale:
——— Public health expenditure/GDP
········· Private health expenditure/GDP
—·—· Total health expenditure/GDP

Right scale:
– – – – · Public health expenditure as % of total public expenditure
– – – Private health expenditure as % of total health expenditure

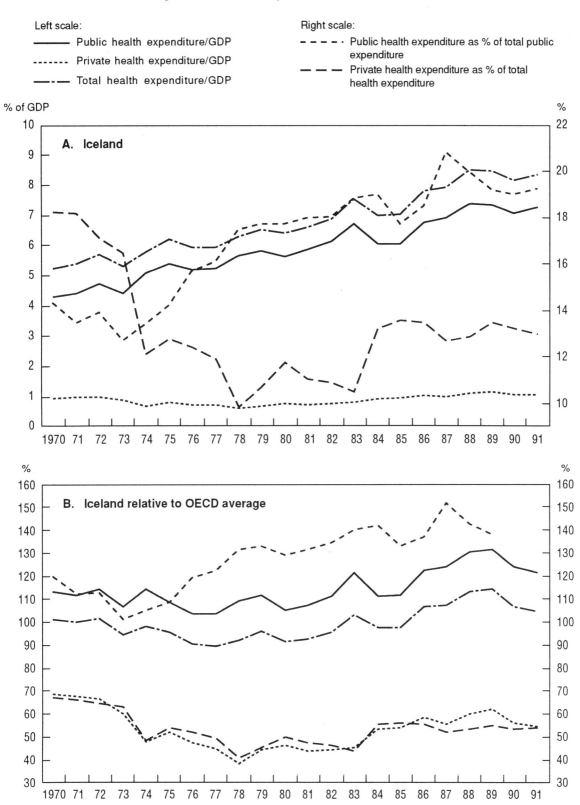

Source: OECD.

75

Table 3.3. **Health care expenditure in Iceland**

Average annual growth rates

	1960-1965	1965-1970	1970-1975	1975-1980	1980-1985	1985-1990[1]	1970-1990[1]
Nominal expenditure							
Total	24.6	20.6	40.5	51.4	54.3	27.2	43.0
Private expenditure	19.4	19.8	30.8	48.9	57.5	27.4	40.6
Inpatient care	24.6	29.7	39.9	60.2	51.8	27.0	44.2
Dental services		35.7	68.6	47.7	51.6	40.1	51.6
Pharmaceutical consumption			43.7	52.6	61.9	28.8	46.2
Real expenditure[2]							
Total	10.9	7.1	9.9	7.5	4.5	5.9	6.9
Private expenditure	6.3	6.4	2.4	5.8	6.6	6.0	5.2
Inpatient care	10.9	15.1	9.5	13.7	2.8	5.7	7.8
Dental services		20.4	31.9	4.9	2.6	16.6	13.4
Pharmaceutical consumption			12.4	8.3	9.7	7.2	9.4
Relative prices[3]							
Total	0.7	0.2	1.8	1.9	−1.4	0.9	0.8
Private expenditure	0.7	0.2	1.8	1.9	−1.4	0.9	0.8
Inpatient care	2.3	−0.7	1.7	1.7	−1.9	1.1	0.6
Dental services	2.3	4.4	−4.8	3.0	−1.6	3.4	−0.1
Pharmaceutical consumption	2.3	−0.7	0.1	2.0	−0.6	0.9	0.6
Volumes[4]							
Total	10.2	6.9	8.0	5.5	6.0	4.9	6.1
Private expenditure	5.6	6.1	0.6	3.7	8.1	5.0	4.3
Inpatient care	8.4	15.9	7.6	11.8	4.8	4.5	7.2
Dental services		15.4	38.5	1.8	4.3	12.7	13.5
Pharmaceutical consumption			12.3	6.2	10.4	6.3	8.7
Volumes per capita[4]							
Total	8.2	5.6	6.6	4.5	4.8	3.7	4.9
Private expenditure	3.8	4.9	−0.8	2.8	6.9	3.8	3.2
Inpatient care	6.5	14.6	6.2	10.8	3.7	3.3	5.9
Dental services		14.0	36.7	0.9	3.1	11.4	12.2
Pharmaceutical consumption			10.8	5.2	9.1	5.0	7.5
Memorandum items:							
Real GDP	7.1	2.4	6.3	6.7	1.7	3.3	4.5
Real GDP per capita	5.2	1.2	4.9	5.8	0.6	2.1	3.3
GDP deflator	12.3	12.7	27.8	40.8	47.7	20.2	33.7

1. Data for 1990 are preliminary.
2. Nominal health-care expenditure divided by the GDP deflator.
3. Medical price deflators divided by the GDP deflator.
4. Real expenditure divided by relative prices, or, equivalently, nominal expenditure divided by the appropriate medical price deflator.
Source: OECD.

real income ranking in that year. This represented 8.4 per cent of GDP, compared to an OECD average of 7.8 per cent (Diagram 3.4). Furthermore, while Iceland's level of per capita real income is among the lowest of the Nordic nations (except Norway), it has had significantly higher per capita medical spending of any except Sweden, as it has since the late 1970s. Part of this can be explained by high medical-care prices in Iceland: on a purchasing-power-parity basis the price level in 1990 was higher than anywhere in the OECD countries except the United States and Switzerland, nearly 10 per cent above the average in the OECD excluding the United States (see Diagram 2.5 in Chapter 2).[11] Drug prices were particularly high due to unusually wide distribution margins at both wholesale and retail levels, and despite low consumption per-capita, drug costs were extremely high in comparison to both Nordic and OECD averages. Once corrected for this price disadvantage, the level of per capita expenditure in volume terms is indeed quite modest, about 15 per cent below the (weighted) OECD average.

While the volume of spending is not far from the OECD average, this is due to offsetting factors. The results of a pooled econometric analysis of health expenditures in the 24 OECD countries during

Diagram 3.3. **Where the money goes**

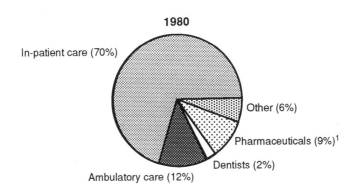

1980

In-patient care (70%)

Other (6%)

Pharmaceuticals (9%)[1]

Dentists (2%)

Ambulatory care (12%)

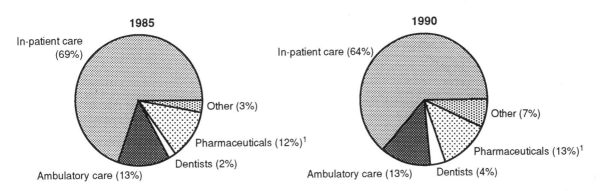

1985

In-patient care (69%)

Other (3%)

Pharmaceuticals (12%)[1]

Dentists (2%)

Ambulatory care (13%)

1990

In-patient care (64%)

Other (7%)

Pharmaceuticals (13%)[1]

Dentists (4%)

Ambulatory care (13%)

1. Includes therapeutic appliances.
Source: OECD.

the period 1985-90 reported in Annex II show that spending is boosted by over a quarter in Iceland compared to the OECD average due to higher levels of real income and somewhat further by a higher share of those under the age of 15 in the population. Higher relative prices of medical care, a higher-than-average public expenditure share, a particularly small share of the population over the age of 65 and a low unemployment rate also serve to reduce expenditure, more than offsetting the usual income-spending relationship.

Over the past thirty years the increase in Iceland's real expenditure on health services has been as rapid as anywhere else among the Nordic and major seven OECD countries except Japan; indeed, since 1975 it has been unsurpassed by any of the major seven (Table 3.4). While some of this gap may be attributable to faster population growth, it represents a small part of the overall story, as even per capita volume growth has outstripped the OECD average by nearly two to one since 1980. Thus, the slowdown remarked upon above has been less significant: the average annual volume growth rate of health expenditure during the fifteen years subsequent to 1975 in the average OECD country slowed much more substantially, compared to the previous fifteen-year period, than did Iceland's. The afore-mentioned trend increase in the relative price of health care has also been more significant for Iceland than for most other OECD countries (Diagram 3.5). However, in recent years price increases have been relatively subdued, especially for drugs. The only exception has been in specialised medical treatment, where the increase in patient costs has been steep.

Diagram 3.4. **Health care expenditures: an international comparison**

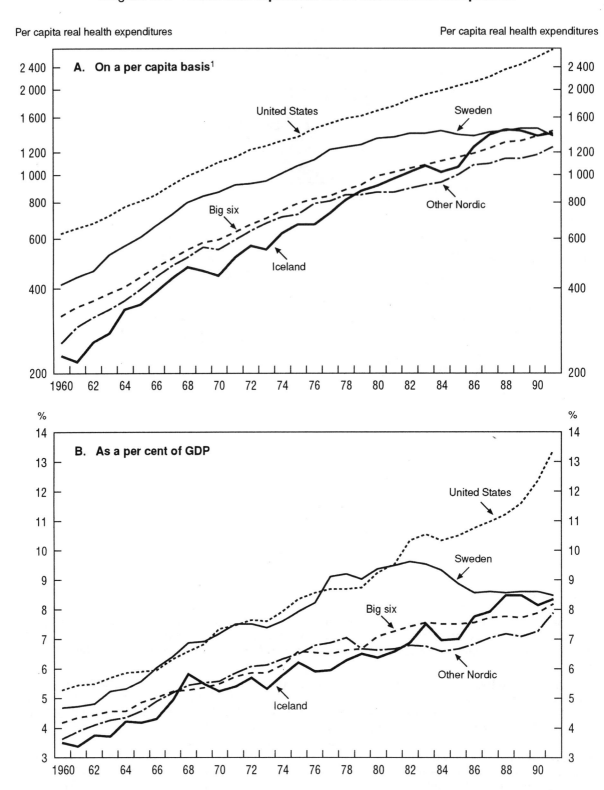

Per capita real health expenditures

Per capita real health expenditures

A. On a per capita basis[1]

United States

Sweden

Big six

Iceland

Other Nordic

B. As a per cent of GDP

United States

Sweden

Big six

Other Nordic

Iceland

1. Expressed in US dollars on a purchasing-power-parity basis and then deflated by the US GDP deflator rebased to 1990.
Source: OECD.

Table 3.4. **Factors in increasing health expenditure in the OECD**

	Share of health expenditure in GDP Starting year	Annual compound rate of growth over ten years							Share of health expenditure in GDP Ending year
		Nominal health expenditure growth	Health care price deflator	of which: GDP deflator	of which: excess health care inflation	Volume growth	of which: population growth	of which: per capita volume intensity growth	
1960 to 1970									
Iceland	3.5	22.6	13.0	12.5	0.4	8.5	1.5	6.9	5.2
Denmark	3.6	17.0	7.0	6.4	0.6	9.3	0.7	8.5	6.1
Finland	3.9	15.2	3.4	5.9	-2.3	11.4	0.4	10.9	5.7
Norway	3.3	13.9	7.6	4.8	2.6	5.8	0.8	5.0	5.0
Sweden	4.7	13.8	3.8	4.3	-0.5	9.7	0.7	8.9	7.2
OECD simple average[1]	3.9	14.4	5.7	4.9	0.8	8.2	1.0	7.2	5.5
1970 to 1980									
Iceland	5.2	45.9	36.7	34.2	1.9	6.7	1.1	5.5	6.4
Denmark	6.1	13.5	8.9	9.7	-0.8	4.2	0.4	3.8	6.8
Finland	5.7	16.9	10.9	11.5	-0.5	5.4	0.4	5.0	6.5
Norway	5.0	16.8	9.3	8.4	0.8	6.9	0.5	6.3	6.6
Sweden	7.2	14.9	11.1	9.6	1.3	3.4	0.3	3.1	9.4
OECD simple average[1]	5.5	18.2	11.7	11.0	0.6	5.8	0.7	5.1	7.2
1980 to 1990[2]									
Iceland	6.4	40.1	32.9	33.4	-0.3	5.4	1.2	4.2	8.3
Denmark	6.8	7.2	6.1	5.7	0.3	1.0	0.0	1.0	6.3
Finland	6.5	12.7	8.8	7.2	1.5	3.5	0.4	3.1	7.8
Norway	6.6	10.0	7.1	6.2	0.8	2.8	0.4	2.4	7.4
Sweden	9.4	8.9	7.1	7.7	-0.6	1.7	0.3	1.4	8.6
OECD simple average[1]	7.2	11.4	8.2	7.7	0.5	2.9	0.5	2.4	7.9

1. Excluding Luxembourg, New Zealand, Portugal and Turkey.
2. Data for 1990 are preliminary.
Source: OECD.

Diagram 3.5. **Trends in the relative price of health care,** [1] **1970-91**

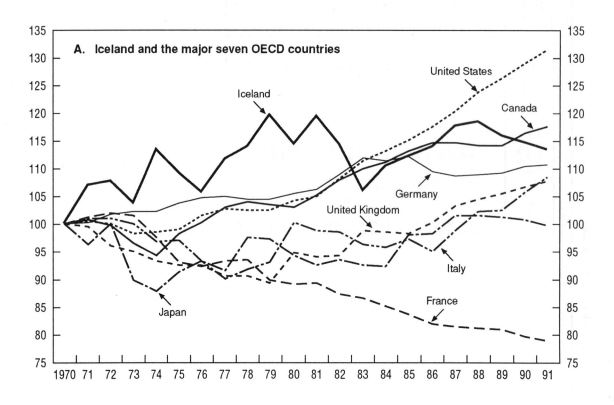

A. **Iceland and the major seven OECD countries**

United States
Iceland
Canada
Germany
United Kingdom
Italy
Japan
France

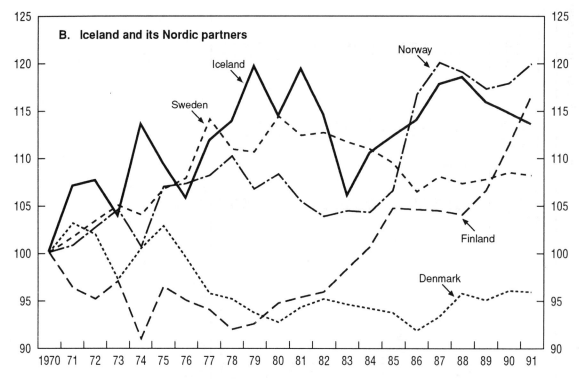

B. **Iceland and its Nordic partners**

Norway
Iceland
Sweden
Finland
Denmark

1. Deflator for health care expenditure divided by the GDP deflator.
Source: OECD.

Aspects of efficiency

Total employment in the health care industry expanded at an average annual rate of 6.3 per cent between 1963 and 1990, reaching about 6½ per cent of total employment in 1990 (Table 3.5). However, this growth slowed to 3.5 per cent between 1980 and 1990, and only 2.9 per cent in the public sector. The fastest rises occurred among nurses. The number of practising physicians per capita also increased steadily, more than doubling in a generation, although the ratio is quite similar to that observed in other Nordic countries. Nonetheless, a further substantial number of Icelandic doctors are practising abroad, especially in Sweden (18 per cent of the total) and the United States (9 per cent), indicating a substantial potential overhang.

In comparison with other OECD countries, Iceland has moved from a position of relatively few health care workers to one of increasing excess. For example, in 1991, Reykjavik's City Hospital had 2.6 full-time equivalent personnel per occupied bed, of which 0.94 nurses, some of the highest staffing ratios in the OECD. However, such a surfeit is not atypical among Nordic countries, especially Sweden. The overabundance is widespread across types of workers, but it is most striking in the case of nurses.[12] While there were 2.1 nurses per practising physician in 1963, by 1989 there were 4.5, and nurses represented 2½ per cent of total employment. A large employment share for health care workers may be to some extent attributable to the sparseness of the rural population. While there have been some signs of the gap with other countries being closed in recent years for physicians (for whom there

Table 3.5. **Employment in health care**

		1963	1973	1980	1985	1990
A.	**In absolute terms**					
	Total	1 655	4 109	6 094	7 395	8 595
	of which:					
	Practising physicians	228	343	488	626	715[1]
	Practising dentists	58	122	168	197	219[1]
	Practising pharmacists	46	100	151	178	210[2]
	Nurses including auxiliary nurses	476	1 188	2 182	2 868	3 200[1]
	Other	847	2 356	3 105	3 526	3 920[2]
	As a percent of total employment	2.3	4.6	5.8	6.1	6.4
B.	**Per thousand inhabitants**					
	Total	8.9	19.3	26.7	30.6	33.6
	of which:					
	Practising physicians	1.2	1.6	2.1	2.6	2.8[1]
	Practising dentists	0.3	0.6	0.7	0.8	0.9[1]
	Practising pharmacists	0.3	0.5	0.7	0.7	0.8[2]
	Nurses including auxiliary nurses	2.6	5.6	9.6	11.9	12.7[1]
	Other	4.6	11.1	13.6	14.6	15.7[2]
C.	**B as a percentage of OECD average**					
	Total	86	123	128	129	136
	of which:					
	Practising physicians	107	113	113	117	113
	Practising dentists	88	138	152	151	144
	Practising pharmacists	75	105	113	114	122
	Nurses including auxiliary nurses	108	– 141	169	185	185
D.	**B as a percentage of Nordic average**[3]					
	Total	61	81	79	82	88
	of which:					
	Physicians	118	108	106	110	101
	Dentists	n.a.	n.a.	99	101	96
	Pharmacists[4]	n.a.	n.a.	92	103	111
	Nurses including auxiliary nurses	n.a.	n.a.	140	148	125

1. 1989.
2. 1988.
3. Excluding Iceland, that is: Denmark, Finland, Norway and Sweden.
4. Excluding Norway. Including Norway the 1990 figure is 124.
Source: OECD.

has been a numerus clausus of 36 graduates per year for some ten years) and dentists, there has been no progress for pharmacists and non-professional categories.

Another aspect of cost efficiency is indicated by the wages and salaries paid to health care workers. The expansion of employment has been offset by a decline in the relative level of labour income per employee in this sector during the 1980s. Over the decade annual earnings fell at an average rate of 0.6 per cent in real terms, while the average employee in the economy saw his yearly compensation rise by 0.2 per cent per year net of inflation. The result was that the relative level of wages per health care employee fell from about 97 per cent of the economy-wide average at the outset of the decade to some 89 per cent by its end. Abroad, health care workers improved their relative position somewhat during the decade (from 90 to 96 per cent). Unfortunately, however, no data on Icelandic doctors' pay levels were available to the OECD at the time of writing, and therefore the importance of their contribution to rising expenditures could not be evaluated.

Other aspects of efficiency relate to the degree to which the available supply of hospital services is fully utilised and the rate of throughput achieved. The number of hospital beds per capita appears at first glance to be rather high by international standards, but once nursing-home beds are excluded,[13] the number of acute-care beds per capita, at 4.8 per thousand in 1989, is in line with the OECD average (4.7). Similarly, occupancy rates at inpatient care institutions is comfortably high (86 per cent in 1989, compared to an average of 81 per cent for 20 other OECD countries), but once attention is restricted to acute-care institutions, the comparison is less favourable (70 per cent in 1989, compared with an average of 77 per cent in eighteen OECD countries). This may well be the result of declining average length of stay achieved during the past two decades: by 1989, the average acute-care patient admitted spent 6.3 days in hospital, the second lowest among 18 OECD countries (the average of which was 8.7 days).

Efficiency can also be judged from the perspective of the minimisation of overhead costs associated with the administration of public health programmes. While international comparisons in this area are fragile because the data are often not gathered according to standardised definitions, it is usually argued that insurance-based ("Bismarckian") systems are more expensive to operate than direct-delivery ("Beveridgean") systems which avoid the costs of premium determination (Poullier, 1992). OECD data tend to confirm this generality (Table 3.6). Indeed, Iceland is among the countries apparently devoting the least both in per capita terms and as a share of total health expenditures to administrative expenses, despite the possible disadvantages of small scale. However, data provided by the national authorities indicate that a broader and possibly more comparable definition would raise the Icelandic figure for administration costs from 1.5 to 2.6 or 2.7 per cent of public expenditure in recent

Table 3.6. **Reported public expenditure on health administration**

	As a share of public expenditure for health (in percent)			In per capita terms (in dollars using purchasing power parity exchange rates for GDP)		
	1980	1985[1]	1990[2]	1980	1985[1]	1990[2]
Iceland	1.5	1.7	1.5	7.9	14.0	18.2
Australia	3.2	2.5	2.6	14.1	17.9	21.6
Belgium	n.a.	5.5	4.6	n.a.	46.0	51.1
Canada	1.2	0.9	n.a.	6.9	9.0	n.a.
Denmark	0.7	0.9	1.3	3.9	6.2	11.1
Finland	2.4	2.5	2.5	10.4	17.2	25.6
Germany	6.1	6.5	7.1	39.2	58.0	77.6
Ireland	2.5	3.7	3.6	9.6	16.9	19.9
Italy	6.6	6.3	6.2	32.3	40.5	62.5
Luxembourg	5.4	5.2	4.8	32.6	43.9	61.3
Netherlands	3.3	4.4	4.5	18.3	31.9	41.0
New Zealand	n.a.	7.0	7.1	n.a.	51.7	54.2
Spain	2.2	2.4	2.8	6.0	9.2	17.4
Switzerland	n.a.	3.2	3.3	4.9	3.8	4.5
United Kingdom	3.0	2.4	n.a.	12.8	14.6	n.a.
United States	3.7	2.7	2.6	16.3	18.9	28.8

1. Except for Belgium and New Zealand for which data are for 1987.
2. Except for Australia, New Zealand and Switzerland for which data are for 1989.
Source: OECD.

years. If internal administrative costs in medical establishments are also included, the figure rises to some 4 per cent.

Finally, efficiency cannot be examined without a look at the role of technology, which poses special problems for an extremely small country such as Iceland. Given the fact that the latest medical advances are usually embodied in new and expensive capital equipment for which demand may not be adequate, the authorities have adopted the sensible policy of sending patients abroad for treatment until domestic needs are sufficient to justify the purchase of such equipment.

Recent and prospective reforms

Faced with the alarming prospect of explosive growth in health care spending in the context of a stagnant economy, the authorities have been actively seeking to reduce the sector's draw on the government budget in recent years. However, there is no desire to reduce the overall level of services provided. Accordingly, the principal focus has been on improving the efficiency of delivery.

As in many other OECD countries, including those in the Nordic region, the principal reform undertaken in the 1980s was the attempt to shift inpatient to ambulatory care in order to save on hospital costs. As shown in Diagram 3.3, after reaching 70 per cent of total health-care spending in 1980, inpatient care's share in expenditure eased back to 65 per cent during the 1980s (56.4 per cent in 1992). As a result of shorter stays, induced by a switch in the late 1970s to financing hospitals through budget envelopes rather than per patient day, this aspect of hospital productivity improved. Hospital costs have also been reduced through rationalisation: the three hospitals in the capital are more specialised than in the past, although a government attempt to merge completely two of them failed in 1992.[14]

In recent years the government has been more energetic in curbing the escalation in public health spending (Table 3.7). Besides an across-the-board cutback in 1992, the most important measures have been to increase financial demands on users, albeit with certain protection provided to the needy.[15] With regard to drugs consumed outside of hospitals, user charges have been increased,[16] and doctors must now indicate to pharmacists whether generic drugs can be substituted for their branded equivalents. This resulted in stability in total expenditure on drugs, a reduced share of costs borne on the health-insurance scheme and prescribing of cheaper medicines. Overall, compared to an extrapolated trend, a saving of Ikr 500 million was realised in the second half of 1991 and Ikr 700 million in 1992. Also, charges have begun to be levied on visits to general practitioners, and those on specialists' as well as dental consultations have been boosted. However, the authorities are not satisfied with the yield of these measures in terms of increases in revenues, reductions in demand for drugs and shifts in demand for physician services,[17] and they intend to increase user charges further. Thus far, the danger in terms of impaired equity of access has not been seen as severe, given the rather flat overall distribution of income in Iceland.

It is also likely that "gate-keeping" will be required on visits to specialists, that is patients will have to be referred by a generalist before an appointment with a specialist can be made. Such a system was

Table 3.7. **Approximate savings from recent measures to cut health expenditures**

Ikr million

	1991	1992	1993
General budget cuts		450	450
Restructuring of acute-care hospitals in Reykjavik		150	150
Other operating savings		200	200
Drugs	500	700	1 100
Primary and outpatient care, especially user charges		250	500
Devices for the handicapped		50	50
Dental services user charges		50	250
Reduction in investment		200	250
Total	500	2 050	2 950

Source: Ministry of Health and Social Security.

in place until 1984. In addition, the authorities continued to impose budget cuts on hospitals in 1993 as in 1992. Enhanced hospital efficiency will be achieved by contracting out a greater share of hospital services, laboratory services, for example, and by further rationalising hospital services in Reykjavik following the failed attempt to merge two of the three biggest hospitals there. Subsidies on devices for the handicapped have been cut back, and capital expenditure is being slowed (especially on nursing homes outside the capital). Finally, greater emphasis is being placed on out-patient clinics, and fewer resources are being allocated to alcohol addiction treatment institutions and rural hospitals (whose surgical role has been diminishing).

However, as yet there appears to have been little willingness to examine other sometimes more radical reforms, and the system remains largely tax-based, publicly owned and operated and organised on a command-and-control basis. For example, there has been no consideration given to schemes which would allow the main hospitals or other providers to compete with one another. Such competition could be based on price, the quality of treatment or the avoidance of queues which have developed in the capital, for example. Encouraging competition could be quite fruitful, especially since it appears that the market for certain inpatient services is currently divided among the hospitals in the capital according to the days of the week. As with all public monopolies, there is a risk of inadequate incentives to improve efficiency and a lack of accountability, with supply guided more by provider than consumer preferences. Somehow, mechanisms must be found to mimic the market, allowing the introduction of the notions of patient choice (of physician and treatment site) and money following the patient. These are completely lacking in the current command-and-control approach in which, for example, hospitals are financed by block grants according to existing supply in order to impose macroeconomic discipline. However, while global budgets can control costs, by themselves they are insufficient to bring about efficient use of resources in the sector, and the injection of competition could yield superior performance.

In addition, the concept of patient choice could be usefully supplemented by contract-based payment systems and performance-related pay. Partial reforms along these lines are underway in other Nordic countries, Sweden in particular (Saltman, 1992),[18] and "health maintenance organisations" (HMOs) and "preferred provider organisations" (PPOs) are gaining support in the United States. Primary-care physicians could be remunerated in part by capitation payments, as in the United Kingdom, or through payments for individual illnesses (so-called "diagnostic-related groups") in order to mitigate the problem of supplier-induced demand. Similarly, it is difficult to understand why price competition is not allowed for pharmaceuticals (whose distribution margins are subject to government control[19]), even for those placed in the category with zero reimbursement. Not surprisingly, the result is substantial mark-ups and high drug prices for Icelandic consumers, as shown above.

The authorities will have to be relentless in their efforts to restrain health expenditure by enhancing efficiency if the weight of evidence from derived historical trends and international comparisons is to be offset. For in the absence of global budgets for all categories of spending, if the true real-income elasticity is in the region of 1.5, as is indicated in Annexes I and II, the relative price of health care services would have to be continuously reduced in order to avoid health occupying an ever-increasing share of GDP.[20] Otherwise, if there is no change in relative prices, health expenditure would constitute about 9.2 per cent of GDP in the year 2000, nearly 1 percentage point higher than in 1990.[21] Global budgets alone could prevent such an increase but at the expense of increased non-price rationing of medical services. In order to cap health spending and simultaneously improve efficiency, global budgets should be supplemented by market-based elements of managed competition.

Notes

1. This is not surprising, as the 1973 Health Services Act guarantees the people of Iceland "access to the best available services to protect and preserve their mental, physical and social health and well-being".

2. About 15 of the rural centres also have a small hospital attached to them, where minor surgical operations are performed.

3. Sweden, in its recent ÄDEL reform, has attempted to integrate primary health and social services for the elderly by unifying responsibility for all such services at the municipal-government level.

4. The most recent data available (1990) show that Icelanders consume only about half as much alcohol per adult as residents of other OECD countries (5.2 litres, compared to 10.2 litres), up from 40 per cent in 1980. However, they consume slightly more tobacco per adult than the OECD average (2.5 kg compared to 2.3 kg).

5. Of course, the main line of causation is probably the reverse: Icelanders consume few pharmaceuticals because they are relatively healthy. In 1988, the average number of medicines taken per person per year in Iceland was 3.3, compared to a simple average for the OECD of 11.3. However, on a defined-daily-dosage basis, Icelanders apparently consume large amounts of psychotropic drugs, antiulcerants and antibiotics compared to their European neighbours.

6. For example, Iceland instituted the OECD's first national screening programme for cervical cancer in 1969 and was, more recently, among the leaders in mammography.

7. However, it is recognised that there is by no means any simple mapping from differences in health care to infant mortality rates across countries: the story is not quite so simple. See Liu *et al.* (1992).

8. The ratio rose to 8.3 per cent in 1993.

9. However, it should be noted that Iceland's health-care system had been less developed than that of many other OECD countries.

10. In 1991, however, there was a sharp drop in pharmaceutical consumption due to an increase in co-payments.

11. Furthermore, unlike in the United States, malpractice insurance is not a contributing factor. Such suits are virtually unheard of in Iceland. The social-security system does, however, have a special account for making lump-sum payments to victims of medical error.

12. Nurses here are defined to include only first- and second-level nurses, that is those with three or two years of post-secondary education. Data gathered by NOMESCO (the Nordic Medico-Statistical Committee) allow for a broader definition of nurses and shows that Iceland has relatively few nurses per doctor by Nordic standards.

13. The excess supply of long-term beds is, in fact, limited to the area outside Reykjavik, while there is an excess demand in the capital.

14. After receiving advice from an international firm of management consultants on the merger of hospitals in Reykjavik, the government attempted unsuccessfully to merge the smaller St. Joseph's Hospital, with the larger and more modern City Hospital, primarily in order to save on overheads. Nevertheless, some degree of rationalisation was achieved, as all acute care was moved from St. Joseph's to the City Hospital.

15. For example, drugs have been almost free since mid-1991 to patients with needs which are expected to exceed six months in duration. It is not clear to what extent increased user charges are intended to mitigate the impact of moral hazard on the demand for health care.

16. 2 000 different drugs are allocated to four different pricing categories, with reimbursement ranging from zero to 100 per cent. In 1991, a fixed fee per prescription was introduced for the largest category, but by 1993, the user charge had been made *ad valorem* at the margin with a reimbursement rate of 75 per cent, provided that the patient charge does not exceed Ikr 3 000 per prescription. For pensioners and the handicapped, the marginal reimbursement rate is 90 per cent, with a ceiling charge of Ikr 800. Over-the-counter drugs, even when prescribed by a physician, and certain other categories of drugs are not reimbursed. A few drugs are fully reimbursed to all. Finally, a "discount card" (available to chronic users) increases the reimbursement rate and lowers the ceiling for some categories. Of course, the higher the reimbursement rate, the higher is the average prescription price observed.

17. Expenditure on specialists' services was substantially beyond budgeted levels in 1992.

18. Admittedly, one cannot neglect the usual Nordic policy maker's rule of thumb that "Sweden reforms first", but there is no reason for undue lags in adopting successful foreign reforms.

19. In 1990, these margins were shaved, saving Ikr 100 million.

20. If the real-income elasticity is 1.5, even with the assumption that the relative-price elasticity is zero, the relative price of health care must fall at half the rate of real GDP growth for the share of health spending in GDP to remain constant. If that assumption is invalid and the elasticity is negative, then the required rate of decline is even greater.

21. This assumes an average growth rate of real GDP of 2 per cent per year.

Bibliography

Arnason, B. (1990), "Heilbrigdisútgjöld 1960-1988", mimeo, May.

Engle, R.F. and C.W.J. Granger (1987), "Co-integration and error-correction: representation, estimation and testing", *Econometrica*, Vol. 55, No. 2, March.

Gerdtham, U., F. Anderson, J. Sogaard and B. Jönsson (1988), "Economic analysis of health care expenditures: a cross-sectional study of OECD countries", *CMT Report*, 1988:9, Centre for Medical Technology Assessment, Linköping, Sweden.

Leu (1986), "The public-private mix and international health care costs", in A.J. Culyer and B. Jönsson, *Public and Private Health Services*.

Liu, K., M. Moon, M. Sulvetta and J. Chawla (1992), "International infant mortality rankings: a look behind the numbers", *Health Care Financing Review*, US Department of Health and Human Services, Vol. 13, No. 4, Summer.

OECD (1990), *Health Care Systems in Transition: the Search for Efficiency*, Paris.

OECD (1991), *Taxing Profits in a Global Economy*, Paris.

Poullier, J.P. (1992), "Administrative costs in selected industrialized countries", *Health Care Financing Review*, Vol. 13, No. 4, Summer.

Saltman, R.B. (1992), "Recent health policy initiatives in Nordic countries", *Health Care Financing Review*, Vol. 13, No. 4, Summer.

Annex I

A time-series estimation of the expenditure on health care in Iceland

This annex presents the results of an attempt to estimate an econometric equation for the demand for health care in Iceland over the past thirty years. The role of population was investigated; specifically, the hypothesis of scale economies was tested. On a per capita basis, demand for health care has been shown to be a well-defined function of real income (*i.e.* real GDP per capita) in a number of other contexts. It is also expected to be negatively related to relative prices, although it is unclear to what extent the price mechanism is allowed to operate in the field of health care and health-care prices are measured rather poorly. Demographic effects may play a significant role: since the aged are more intensive users of the health-care system, the volume of health-care expenditures per capita should be positively related to the proportion of the population over 65. Other evidence has pointed to a positive impact coming from the youth share as well; accordingly, the share of the population under the age of 15 is included in the list of regressors. Finally, there may well be cyclical variations in the demand for medical care, as the unemployed could be less healthy than their employed counterparts. They would also have a lower shadow price of queuing for rationed care. Thus, a higher unemployment rate could be associated with a greater volume expenditure on health care.

Data are available for Iceland's health spending and other needed variables from 1960 to 1990. In preliminary estimation an effort was made to see if any of the aforementioned regressors might appear with a lag; the only support came from the relative price term. Thus, estimation proceeded over the period 1961 to 1990. The equation was specified in double-logarithmic form, except for the demographic variables and the unemployment rate, which are already in share form. For the latter in fact, both functional forms were tested and were seen to have separate effects. Last, there were no significant departures from constant returns to population growth, and the per-capita specification was adopted. The resulting estimation outcome is given below (with absolute values of t-ratios in parentheses*):

ln(Real health spending per capita) = 0.02 + 1.72*ln(Real GDP per capita)
$\qquad\qquad$ (0.02) (6.44)

$-$ 0.98*ln(Relative price) + 0.73*ln(Lagged relative price) + 0.22*Share > 65
(2.59) $\qquad\qquad\qquad$ (2.58) $\qquad\qquad\qquad\qquad$ (2.25)

$-$ 0.93*Share < 15 + 0.20*ln(Unemployment rate) $-$ 0.13*Unemployment rate $\qquad$ [1]
(2.99) $\qquad\qquad$ (5.02) $\qquad\qquad\qquad\qquad$ (2.30)

Adjusted R2 = 0.9913 $\quad$ SEE = 0.0475 $\quad$ DW = 1.78

SEE = Standard Error of Estimate; $\qquad$ DW = Durbin and Watson

The results largely conform to our expectations, except that the youth share has a significantly negative coefficient. Furthermore, the hypothesis that the long-run effect of relative prices is zero cannot be rejected. With this constraint as well as the elimination of the insignificant constant term, the following result is derived:

ln(Real health spending per capita) = 1.62*ln(Real GDP per capita)
$\qquad\qquad$ (11.92)

$-$ 0.82*ln(Relative price/lagged relative price) + 0.24*Share > 65
(3.75) $\qquad\qquad\qquad\qquad\qquad\qquad$ (2.91)

$-$ 0.93*Share < 15 + 0.20*ln(Unemployment rate) $-$ 0.13*Unemployment rate $\qquad$ [2]
(9.53) $\qquad\qquad$ (5.76) $\qquad\qquad$. $\qquad\qquad$ (2.54)

Adjusted R2 = 0.9919 $\quad$ SEE = 0.0459 $\quad$ DW = 1.65

The results show that the real income elasticity is likely to be around 1.6. This is similar to the findings of Arnason (1990), but somewhat higher than most estimates for other countries which are in the 1.0 to 1.5 range (OECD, 1990, p. 31). Second, prices probably only have a short-run effect, but whatever long-run influence they have is quite small. Third, demographic effects appear to be important: fewer youths and more elderly both serve to raise health expenditure levels. Finally, the impact of unemployment seems to be non-linear: higher unemployment

---

* The t-ratios reported in equations [1] and [2] should be interpreted with caution; since real per capita health spending is non-stationary, they are not typically t-distributed. Co-integration tests are discussed below.

rates raise health spending, as posited, but only until the rate reaches 0.20/0.13, that is slightly over 1½ per cent, a value reached only occasionally over the historical period.

However, some of these conclusions may not be robust, since real health-care spending per capita is non-stationary, and thus the t-ratios may not be interpretable (Engle and Granger, 1987). Indeed, the Engle-Granger test for co-integration led to inconclusive results, with a confidence level of only some 80 per cent that the equation residuals are stationary.

Accordingly, the matter was pursued further, and both long- and short-run relationships were specified. In the first long-run (levels) estimation, the terms in unemployment and in the youth share were eliminated, and the equation was rerun, but the results were even less satisfactory from the perspective of the Engle-Granger co-integration test. A search for other non-stationary variables which might have been omitted (besides a deterministic trend, which was highly collinear with the other included regressors), turned up a significant shift variable on real income per capita. With such a long-run specification, the co-integration test outcome was very similar to the 80 per cent confidence level reported above, but inclusion of the lagged residual in the short-run equation yielded a totally insignificant parameter estimate, whereas inclusion of the residual from the original equation [2] yielded the sought-after significant negative parameter estimate given below:

dln(Real health spending per capita) = 0.76*dln(Real GDP per capita)
                                        (6.59)

+ 0.76*dln(Lagged real GDP per capita) − 0.85*dln(Relative price)
  (6.59)   (3.13)

+ 0.06*dln(Unemployment rate) + 0.09*D − 0.66*Residuals   [3]
  (2.88)   (3.16)   (2.96)

Adjusted R2 = 0.5385   SEE = 0.0455   DW = 1.95

where D is a dummy variable for the period up to 1964 and the residuals are from equation [2].

To sum up then, it can be said that: a) the long-term real-income elasticity is likely to be in the range of 1½ to 1¾, only slightly above the short-run elasticity; b) the short-run relative-price elasticity is probably in the range of 0.6 to 1.1, but the longer-run value may very well be zero; c) the share of the elderly does have a significant long-run influence, with a semi-elasticity of about one-quarter; d) it is uncertain whether there is a long-run influence from the youth share; and e) increases in the unemployment rate may have a long-run positive impact, but only over a certain range and only, of course, if the rate is non-stationary; in any case there is a short-run effect, with a ten per cent (not percentage point) increase in the rate of joblessness associated with a 0.6 per cent rise in the volume of per capita health-care spending.

A pooled approach to health care spending in 24 OECD countries

A further effort has been made by the OECD's Secretariat to determine the factors which explain the cross-country pattern of health care expenditure in order to isolate those which distinguish Iceland's case from others in the OECD.

Initially, the model was specified for the year 1990, but eventually, in order to make maximum use of the available data, a pooled cross-country time-series approach was used.* Health-care spending, expressed in dollars at purchasing power parity (PPP) exchange rates for household consumption expenditure on medical and health care, was assumed to be a function of the following factors:

1. Real income per capita translated into dollars using PPP exchange rates for GDP. Nearly all previous evidence points to an estimated elasticity in excess of unity; indeed, the time-series estimate for Iceland derived in Annex I was above 1.5.
2. Population. Naturally, the greater is the population, the more the country is likely to spend on health care. More interesting is whether or not the elasticity is equal to unity, that is, are there economies or diseconomies of scale to larger populations?
3. Relative prices, defined to be the price of medical and health-care consumption divided by the price of overall GDP, both from the PPP data base. If indeed prices are an effective rationing mechanism in the medical sphere, then this term should exert downward pressure on the volume of health-care spending.
4. The share of the population over 65. Age is probably the most influential factor in determining the level of drug consumption – for example, 70 year-old men use about 4½ times as many pharmaceutical items as their 40 year-old counterparts. Overall, elderly Americans need about four times as much medical care as the rest of the population. If this ratio is borne out elsewhere, then a 1 percentage point increase in the elderly share of the population should be associated with a 3 per cent increase in (per capita) health spending.
5. The share of the population under 15. Some previous research has shown that the young have significantly higher health care needs (Leu, 1986), while others (Gerdtham *et al.*, 1988) have found the opposite. The difference may be due to very high expenditure in the first year of life.
6. The share of public financing in total heath expenditure. What has become known in the literature as the "public-choice view" of international differences in health expenditure (OECD, 1990) posits that public finance increases demand by reducing the user price to the consumer and likewise increases supply as necessary to meet the extra demand.
7. The unemployment rate. Higher unemployment might induce more psychosomatic and other illness and will bring down the shadow price of queueing for rationed health care.

The equation was specified in double logarithmic form except for those regressors which are expressed in share terms (4 to 7 above). In preliminary estimation checks were made as to the possibility of time-varying parameters; the only variable manifesting such an effect was the real income variable. The estimation results are given below (with absolute values of t-ratios in parentheses):

ln(Health expenditure in PPP dollars) = − 3.94 + 1.60*ln(Real income per capita
$\qquad\qquad\qquad\qquad\qquad\qquad\quad$ (16.45) (38.53)

in PPP dollars) − 0.0086*TIME*ln(Real income per capita in PPP dollars)
$\qquad\qquad\qquad$ (3.45)

\+ 0.97*ln(Population) − 1.03*ln(Relative prices) + 0.03*Share > 65
(102.0) $\qquad\qquad\qquad$ (13.35) $\qquad\qquad\qquad$ (4.59)

\+ 0.02*Share < 15 − 0.0087*Public expenditure share + 0.0084*Unemployment rate
(3.40) $\qquad\qquad$ (6.32) $\qquad\qquad\qquad\qquad\qquad$ (3.08)

R^2 = 0.9962 $\qquad$ SEE = 0.1043 $\qquad$ Number of observations = 144

where TIME is unity in 1985 and is incremented annually.

---

* All data are available on a time-series basis for the period 1985-90 except health care prices which are only available for the years 1985 and 1990. Thus, data for this series for the intervening years were obtained by interpolation.

These results reveal that the real income elasticity is indeed in excess of 1.5, but also that it has had some tendency to decline very slightly during the last half of the 1980s. Furthermore, the equation is properly specified in absolute rather than per capita terms, as there is significant evidence of some limited economies of scale – the t-ratio for the test of whether the parameter on the population variable differs from unity is 3.82. A third very tentative conclusion is that there may be a significant role for relative prices in rationing the demand for health care. However, this unitary estimated elasticity may be reflecting, even in a cross-country context, the constraint of fixed health care budgets in most OECD countries: higher prices may be inevitably offset by lower volumes on the supply side even if there is no reaction on the demand side. Alternatively, if the price level of total health expenditure is better proxied by the PPP for total expenditure on GDP than by the PPP for household consumption of medical and health care used here, there would be a clear bias toward this result. Demographics are also important. As expected, the elderly are seen to consume about four times as much in the way of health services as the rest of the population, while the young also consume significantly more (as Leu, 1986, had found). In addition, public financing is associated with less spending, not more as supporters of the public-choice view contend. Finally, higher unemployment is associated with higher health-care spending: each percentage point raises outlays by nearly 1 per cent.

The equation results have been used for two further pieces of analysis. First, they have been exploited to generate the predicted evolution of health spending in volume terms in Iceland over the estimation period. The results are given below in logarithmic differences times 100 (which approximate growth rates in per cent):

	Predicted	Actual
1986	15.1	19.4
1987	12.9	12.7
1988	1.3	9.8
1989	5.1	4.4
1990	5.9	2.4

Therefore, spending growth was "surprisingly" strong in 1986 and, especially, in 1988, before moderating more than expected in 1989 and, especially, in 1990. The vast majority of the slowdown is the result of the stagnation in real per capita incomes, while movements in the unemployment rate and in the youth share have tended to soften that outcome.

Second, averages of the vectors of explanatory variables across the six-year sample period were calculated in order to explore the relative importance of the different factors in determining the level of Iceland's spending. Of course, the dominant factor is population, but once this is controlled for, Icelanders spent 4.2 per cent less than the average OECD country when expenditure is evaluated in terms of expenditure-specific PPP price levels. The equation allocates this as follows:

Real income per capita	+25.9	Public expenditure share	−10.6
Share < 15	+7.6	Share > 65	−8.1
Unexplained residual	+5.0	Unemployment rate	−5.2
		Relative prices	−0.5

Thus, higher real incomes are the single most important factor in determining differences in spending patterns between Iceland and the average OECD country. Outlays are also boosted by the large share of the population under 15. Offsetting these factors are the restraining effects of the high relative price of health care, of the higher-than-average public expenditure share, of the small share of the population over 65 and of the low unemployment rate. Overall, though, spending in the second half of the 1980s was nearly 5 per cent higher than predicted by the equation.

MAIN SALES OUTLETS OF OECD PUBLICATIONS
PRINCIPAUX POINTS DE VENTE DES PUBLICATIONS DE L'OCDE

ARGENTINA – ARGENTINE
Carlos Hirsch S.R.L.
Galería Güemes, Florida 165, 4° Piso
1333 Buenos Aires   Tel. (1) 331.1787 y 331.2391
Telefax: (1) 331.1787

AUSTRALIA – AUSTRALIE
D.A. Information Services
648 Whitehorse Road, P.O.B 163
Mitcham, Victoria 3132   Tel. (03) 873.4411
Telefax: (03) 873.5679

AUSTRIA – AUTRICHE
Gerold & Co.
Graben 31
Wien I   Tel. (0222) 533.50.14

BELGIUM – BELGIQUE
Jean De Lannoy
Avenue du Roi 202
B-1060 Bruxelles   Tel. (02) 538.51.69/538.08.41
Telefax: (02) 538.08.41

CANADA
Renouf Publishing Company Ltd.
1294 Algoma Road
Ottawa, ON K1B 3W8   Tel. (613) 741.4333
Telefax: (613) 741.5439
Stores:
61 Sparks Street
Ottawa, ON K1P 5R1   Tel. (613) 238.8985
211 Yonge Street
Toronto, ON M5B 1M4   Tel. (416) 363.3171
Telefax: (416)363.59.63
Les Éditions La Liberté Inc.
3020 Chemin Sainte-Foy
Sainte-Foy, PQ G1X 3V6   Tel. (418) 658.3763
Telefax: (418) 658.3763

Federal Publications Inc.
165 University Avenue, Suite 701
Toronto, ON M5H 3B8   Tel. (416) 860.1611
Telefax: (416) 860.1608
Les Publications Fédérales
1185 Université
Montréal, QC H3B 3A7   Tel. (514) 954.1633
Telefax : (514) 954.1635

CHINA – CHINE
China National Publications Import
Export Corporation (CNPIEC)
16 Gongti E. Road, Chaoyang District
P.O. Box 88 or 50
Beijing 100704 PR   Tel. (01) 506.6688
Telefax: (01) 506.3101

**CZECH REPUBLIC – RÉPUBLIQUE
TCHÈQUE**
Artia Pegas Press Ltd.
Narodni Trida 25
POB 825
111 21 Praha 1   Tel. 26.65.68
Telefax: 26.20.81

DENMARK – DANEMARK
Munksgaard Book and Subscription Service
35, Nørre Søgade, P.O. Box 2148
DK-1016 København K   Tel. (33) 12.85.70
Telefax: (33) 12.93.87

EGYPT – ÉGYPTE
Middle East Observer
41 Sherif Street
Cairo   Tel. 392.6919
Telefax: 360-6804

FINLAND – FINLANDE
Akateeminen Kirjakauppa
Keskuskatu 1, P.O. Box 128
00100 Helsinki
Subscription Services/Agence d'abonnements :
P.O. Box 23
00371 Helsinki   Tel. (358 0) 12141
Telefax: (358 0) 121.4450

FRANCE
OECD/OCDE
Mail Orders/Commandes par correspondance:
2, rue André-Pascal
75775 Paris Cedex 16   Tel. (33-1) 45.24.82.00
Telefax: (33-1) 49.10.42.76
Telex: 640048 OCDE
Orders via Minitel, France only/
Commandes par Minitel, France exclusivement :
36 15 OCDE

OECD Bookshop/Librairie de l'OCDE :
33, rue Octave-Feuillet
75016 Paris   Tel. (33-1) 45.24.81.67
(33-1) 45.24.81.81

Documentation Française
29, quai Voltaire
75007 Paris   Tel. 40.15.70.00

Gibert Jeune (Droit-Économie)
6, place Saint-Michel
75006 Paris   Tel. 43.25.91.19

Librairie du Commerce International
10, avenue d'Iéna
75016 Paris   Tel. 40.73.34.60

Librairie Dunod
Université Paris-Dauphine
Place du Maréchal de Lattre de Tassigny
75016 Paris   Tel. (1) 44.05.40.13

Librairie Lavoisier
11, rue Lavoisier
75008 Paris   Tel. 42.65.39.95

Librairie L.G.D.J. - Montchrestien
20, rue Soufflot
75005 Paris   Tel. 46.33.89.85

Librairie des Sciences Politiques
30, rue Saint-Guillaume
75007 Paris   Tel. 45.48.36.02

P.U.F.
49, boulevard Saint-Michel
75005 Paris   Tel. 43.25.83.40

Librairie de l'Université
12a, rue Nazareth
13100 Aix-en-Provence   Tel. (16) 42.26.18.08

Documentation Française
165, rue Garibaldi
69003 Lyon   Tel. (16) 78.63.32.23

Librairie Decitre
29, place Bellecour
69002 Lyon   Tel. (16) 72.40.54.54

GERMANY – ALLEMAGNE
OECD Publications and Information Centre
August-Bebel-Allee 6
D-53175 Bonn   Tel. (0228) 959.120
Telefax: (0228) 959.12.17

GREECE – GRÈCE
Librairie Kauffmann
Mavrokordatou 9
106 78 Athens   Tel. (01) 32.55.321
Telefax: (01) 36.33.967

HONG-KONG
Swindon Book Co. Ltd.
13–15 Lock Road
Kowloon, Hong Kong   Tel. 2376.2062
Telefax: 2376.0685

HUNGARY – HONGRIE
Euro Info Service
Margitsziget, Európa Ház
1138 Budapest   Tel. (1) 111.62.16
Telefax : (1) 111.60.61

ICELAND – ISLANDE
Mál Mog Menning
Laugavegi 18, Pósthólf 392
121 Reykjavik   Tel. 162.35.23

INDIA – INDE
Oxford Book and Stationery Co.
Scindia House
New Delhi 110001   Tel.(11) 331.5896/5308
Telefax: (11) 332.5993
17 Park Street
Calcutta 700016   Tel. 240832

INDONESIA – INDONÉSIE
Pdii-Lipi
P.O. Box 4298
Jakarta 12042   Tel. (21) 573.34.67
Telefax: (21) 573.34.67

IRELAND – IRLANDE
Government Supplies Agency
Publications Section
4/5 Harcourt Road
Dublin 2   Tel. 661.31.11
Telefax: 478.06.45

ISRAEL
Praedicta
5 Shatner Street
P.O. Box 34030
Jerusalem 91430   Tel. (2) 52.84.90/1/2
Telefax: (2) 52.84.93
R.O.Y.
P.O. Box 13056
Tel Aviv 61130   Tél. (3) 49.61.08
Telefax (3) 544.60.39

ITALY – ITALIE
Libreria Commissionaria Sansoni
Via Duca di Calabria 1/1
50125 Firenze   Tel. (055) 64.54.15
Telefax: (055) 64.12.57
Via Bartolini 29
20155 Milano   Tel. (02) 36.50.83
Editrice e Libreria Herder
Piazza Montecitorio 120
00186 Roma   Tel. 679.46.28
Telefax: 678.47.51
Libreria Hoepli
Via Hoepli 5
20121 Milano   Tel. (02) 86.54.46
Telefax: (02) 805.28.86
Libreria Scientifica
Dott. Lucio de Biasio 'Aeiou'
Via Coronelli, 6
20146 Milano   Tel. (02) 48.95.45.52
Telefax: (02) 48.95.45.48

JAPAN – JAPON
OECD Publications and Information Centre
Landic Akasaka Building
2-3-4 Akasaka, Minato-ku
Tokyo 107   Tel. (81.3) 3586.2016
Telefax: (81.3) 3584.7929

KOREA – CORÉE
Kyobo Book Centre Co. Ltd.
P.O. Box 1658, Kwang Hwa Moon
Seoul   Tel. 730.78.91
Telefax: 735.00.30

MALAYSIA – MALAISIE
University of Malaya Bookshop
University of Malaya
P.O. Box 1127, Jalan Pantai Baru
59700 Kuala Lumpur
Malaysia   Tel. 756.5000/756.5425
Telefax: 756.3246

MEXICO – MEXIQUE
Revistas y Periodicos Internacionales S.A. de C.V.
Florencia 57 - 1004
Mexico, D.F. 06600   Tel. 207.81.00
Telefax : 208.39.79

NETHERLANDS – PAYS-BAS
SDU Uitgeverij Plantijnstraat
Externe Fondsen
Postbus 20014
2500 EA's-Gravenhage   Tel. (070) 37.89.880
Voor bestellingen: Telefax: (070) 34.75.778

NEW ZEALAND
NOUVELLE-ZÉLANDE
Legislation Services
P.O. Box 12418
Thorndon, Wellington   Tel. (04) 496.5652
   Telefax: (04) 496.5698

NORWAY – NORVÈGE
Narvesen Info Center – NIC
Bertrand Narvesens vei 2
P.O. Box 6125 Etterstad
0602 Oslo 6   Tel. (022) 57.33.00
   Telefax: (022) 68.19.01

PAKISTAN
Mirza Book Agency
65 Shahrah Quaid-E-Azam
Lahore 54000   Tel. (42) 353.601
   Telefax: (42) 231.730

PHILIPPINE – PHILIPPINES
International Book Center
5th Floor, Filipinas Life Bldg.
Ayala Avenue
Metro Manila   Tel. 81.96.76
   Telex 23312 RHP PH

PORTUGAL
Livraria Portugal
Rua do Carmo 70-74
Apart. 2681
1200 Lisboa   Tel.: (01) 347.49.82/5
   Telefax: (01) 347.02.64

SINGAPORE – SINGAPOUR
Gower Asia Pacific Pte Ltd.
Golden Wheel Building
41, Kallang Pudding Road, No. 04-03
Singapore 1334   Tel. 741.5166
   Telefax: 742.9356

SPAIN – ESPAGNE
Mundi-Prensa Libros S.A.
Castelló 37, Apartado 1223
Madrid 28001   Tel. (91) 431.33.99
   Telefax: (91) 575.39.98

Libreria Internacional AEDOS
Consejo de Ciento 391
08009 – Barcelona   Tel. (93) 488.30.09
   Telefax: (93) 487.76.59

Llibreria de la Generalitat
Palau Moja
Rambla dels Estudis, 118
08002 – Barcelona
   (Subscripcions) Tel. (93) 318.80.12
   (Publicacions) Tel. (93) 302.67.23
   Telefax: (93) 412.18.54

SRI LANKA
Centre for Policy Research
c/o Colombo Agencies Ltd.
No. 300-304, Galle Road
Colombo 3   Tel. (1) 574240, 573551-2
   Telefax: (1) 575394, 510711

SWEDEN – SUÈDE
Fritzes Information Center
Box 16356
Regeringsgatan 12
106 47 Stockholm   Tel. (08) 690.90.90
   Telefax: (08) 20.50.21

Subscription Agency/Agence d'abonnements :
Wennergren-Williams Info AB
P.O. Box 1305
171 25 Solna   Tel. (08) 705.97.50
   Téléfax : (08) 27.00.71

SWITZERLAND – SUISSE
Maditec S.A. (Books and Periodicals - Livres
et périodiques)
Chemin des Palettes 4
Case postale 266
1020 Renens VD 1   Tel. (021) 635.08.65
   Telefax: (021) 635.07.80

Librairie Payot S.A.
4, place Pépinet
CP 3212
1002 Lausanne   Tel. (021) 341.33.47
   Telefax: (021) 341.33.45

Librairie Unilivres
6, rue de Candolle
1205 Genève   Tel. (022) 320.26.23
   Telefax: (022) 329.73.18

Subscription Agency/Agence d'abonnements :
Dynapresse Marketing S.A.
38 avenue Vibert
1227 Carouge   Tel.: (022) 308.07.89
   Telefax : (022) 308.07.99

See also – Voir aussi :
OECD Publications and Information Centre
August-Bebel-Allee 6
D-53175 Bonn (Germany)   Tel. (0228) 959.120
   Telefax: (0228) 959.12.17

TAIWAN – FORMOSE
Good Faith Worldwide Int'l. Co. Ltd.
9th Floor, No. 118, Sec. 2
Chung Hsiao E. Road
Taipei   Tel. (02) 391.7396/391.7397
   Telefax: (02) 394.9176

THAILAND – THAÏLANDE
Suksit Siam Co. Ltd.
113, 115 Fuang Nakhon Rd.
Opp. Wat Rajbopith
Bangkok 10200   Tel. (662) 225.9531/2
   Telefax: (662) 222.5188

TURKEY – TURQUIE
Kültür Yayinlari Is-Türk Ltd. Sti.
Atatürk Bulvari No. 191/Kat 13
Kavaklidere/Ankara   Tel. 428.11.40 Ext. 2458
Dolmabahce Cad. No. 29
Besiktas/Istanbul   Tel. 260.71.88
   Telex: 43482B

UNITED KINGDOM – ROYAUME-UNI
HMSO
Gen. enquiries   Tel. (071) 873 0011
Postal orders only:
P.O. Box 276, London SW8 5DT
Personal Callers HMSO Bookshop
49 High Holborn, London WC1V 6HB
   Telefax: (071) 873 8200
Branches at: Belfast, Birmingham, Bristol, Edin-
burgh, Manchester

UNITED STATES – ÉTATS-UNIS
OECD Publications and Information Centre
2001 L Street N.W., Suite 700
Washington, D.C. 20036-4910 Tel. (202) 785.6323
   Telefax: (202) 785.0350

VENEZUELA
Libreria del Este
Avda F. Miranda 52, Aptdo. 60337
Edificio Galipán
Caracas 106   Tel. 951.1705/951.2307/951.1297
   Telegram: Libreste Caracas

Subscription to OECD periodicals may also be placed through main subscription agencies.

Les abonnements aux publications périodiques de l'OCDE peuvent être souscrits auprès des principales agences d'abonnement.

Orders and inquiries from countries where Distributors have not yet been appointed should be sent to: OECD Publications Service, 2 rue André-Pascal, 75775 Paris Cedex 16, France.

Les commandes provenant de pays où l'OCDE n'a pas encore désigné de distributeur peuvent être adressées à : OCDE, Service des Publications, 2, rue André-Pascal, 75775 Paris Cedex 16, France.

1-1995

OECD PUBLICATIONS, 2 rue André-Pascal, 75775 PARIS CEDEX 16
PRINTED IN FRANCE
(81 95 03 1) ISBN 92-64-14339-4 - No. 47691 1995